AFTER THE FREEZE

A teacher's adventure

in

Cossack Russia

By

Gilli Robson

Gilli Robson, a 49 year old mother of two, decided to teach English to speakers of other languages and have an adventure abroad. She was offered a job in Southwest Russia near the Black Sea and taught there from Winter 1996 to Summer 1999. This was a period of confusion and economic collapse in Russia.

Her humorous, down to earth, and life-affirming "tell-it-like-it-is" story documents the very human drama and genuine care of people she encountered who, despite real and pressing challenges, responded in ways that inspire and uplift the human spirit.

Many of the author's experiences are extremely funny and she is not afraid of showing herself in a ridiculous light.

A must read for anyone who values the very human craving for adventure and inspiration.

Copyright © Gilli Robson 2018
ISBN: 9781983112157
Imprint: Independently published
Cover and book design by Sreeram Iyer

To my Russian friends

You can't just sit there and wait for success to fall into your lap; once your course is set and your will is firm, you have to make a practical effort. Then you will see that whatever you require for success starts coming to you. Everything will push you in the right direction. In your divinely surcharged will power is the answer to prayer. When you use that will, you open the way through which your prayers can be answered.

You think you must have this or that and then you can be happy. But no matter how many of your desires are satisfied, you never will find happiness through them. The more you have, the more you want. Learn to live simply.

Paramahansa Yogananda,
Man's Eternal Quest

CONTENTS

PREFACE 8

1 PREPARATION 12

MAP OF MY ADVENTURE IN
SOUTHWEST RUSSIA 18

3 FIRST DAYS 26

4 PAUL 36

5 TAGANROG TOWN AND PEOPLE 42

6 THE COSSACKS 55

7 HOSPITAL 60

8 MOSCOW 66

9 GOODBYE ROSA LUXEMBURG 81

10 OUR FIRST MOVE 86

11 THE CAUCASUS 90

12 THE REPUBLIC OF GEORGIA 96

13 WE MOVE AGAIN 112

14 ICE ON LAND AND SEA 119

15 CHRISTMAS AND NEW YEAR 127

16 DOGS, DOGS, DOGS 131

17 EDUCATION 140

18 THE HOLIDAY THAT WASN'T 149

19 DIFFICULT DAYS 155

20 THE WEDDING 162

21 HARD TIMES 169

22 ALL CHANGE 178

23 ST PETERSBURG...185

24 THE ECONOMIC CRISIS BITES........................194

25 THE COST OF LIVING......................................206

26 MUSIC AND DANCE 209

27 THE ENGLISH CLUB..214

28 PEOPLE, PARTIES AND PUBLIC HOLIDAYS 221

29 TRIPS OUT OF TOWN.....................................231

30 WATER, WATER EVERYWHERE,
   AND NOT A DROP TO WASH IN....................247

31 THE FRIDGE SAGA..253

32 I HATE TO SAY GOODBYE..............................262

33 FAREWELL, RUSSIA..278

EPILOGUE..278

Preface

Living and working in a foreign country is a challenge, and can be a way of highlighting one's talents and one's faults, as one is freed from the normal routine and expectations of those who know you well. This book is based upon the diary I kept for the best part of three years in south-west Russia, from 1996 to 1999.

I have endeavoured to be honest, and do not always show up in a good light. There are times when I shudder as I read this, and wonder at my arrogance! There are also moments when I laugh outright. One thing I do know for sure: those three years taught me a great deal.

To protect the privacy of the many people I met, I have only used their familiar first names. In some cases I have changed that name completely for the sake of readers, as too many Olgas and Katyas can be confusing.

I believe it might be helpful here to provide a very brief history leading up to 1996, as this was a time of great change in Russia.

In 1985, the Russian president, Mikhail Gorbachev, introduced *perestroika* and *glasnost*. The former consisted of plans for a hybrid communist/capitalist system, giving less power to the Central Planning Committee, and more power to market forces. Gorbachev also envisioned a democratically elected Communist Party with many more young representatives. *Glasnost* aimed to give the people more freedom, in terms of speech, publication, the Press and religion.

The Western nations were generally delighted at the prospect of such reforms, but many people in Russia – particularly the older generation – felt threatened by what they perceived as a weakened and vulnerable government. One must remember that this huge 'empire' had been ruled by autocrats of one sort or another for hundreds of years.

From 1989, nationalist movements - particularly in the outlying satellites in Eastern Europe – began to break away, starting with Poland, and rapidly extending to East Germany, Czechoslovakia, Yugoslavia, Hungary, the Ukraine, Belarus and, finally, the Baltic States.

The central government was not strong enough, nor was the economy healthy enough, to halt this trend, and the old Soviet Union was greatly reduced by 1991.

In the early 1990s, various changes in the way the economy was run led to near-bankruptcy of Russian industry and a severe drop in living standards. Many families lost all their savings as banks collapsed. Of course, there were winners too. There always are in difficult times. These were mostly young entrepreneurs and black marketeers.

In August 1991, while Gorbachev was holidaying in the Crimea with his family, there was a military coup in Moscow led by hardline communists. However, this was resisted by those who were unwilling to lose their newfound freedom. The army changed sides, and supported Yeltsin, who banned the Communist Party and accepted the break-up of the old Soviet Union.

By November 1996, when I started teaching in south-west Russia, the communist system was in a state of collapse, while a capitalist system was by no means firmly established.

Many older people grieved for the loss of a system that ensured free or very cheap travel throughout the old Soviet Union, cheap holiday camps for their children during the long summer months, and full employment. The younger generation, on the other hand, welcomed the opening up of communication with the outside world and the possibility of starting successful businesses unhampered by Soviet bureaucracy.

Ironically, as my friend Vladimir told me in 1999, Russian people were now in a position to learn what was happening in the outside world and to follow new inventions and projects in other countries, but at the same time they hadn't enough money to travel outside Russia and meet up with the scientists and innovators they now knew about. In this atmosphere of insecurity and confusion, Yeltsin was becoming unpopular.

It was certainly an interesting time to be living in Russia.

1 Preparation

"You have what they call the itchy feet," she said, her sharp but kindly eyes drilling into mine. "There'll be times when you'll be wantin' to leave your family and friends and go far, far away. But you won't, or not whiles they need you. Because you love them, so you do." Other things she said too, that wise old woman in a tatty caravan beside the entrance of an Aberdeenshire fair. And my 7-year-old son and his friend sat as quiet as mice, their eyes wide as goblets, squashed side by side on a small seat in the caravan. All ears. It was they who had begged me to have my fortune told. "Oh please, please. And can we listen." When I asked the old woman if the boys could come in too, she agreed, with the proviso – of course – that certain things she might not feel free to say in their hearing.

That was many years ago, but I never forgot her words, which lay at the circumference of my mind, waiting to be acknowledged. For the truth was that, ever since I had been sent to a boarding school in England to complete my studies in the sixth form, leaving my beloved Kenya, I had felt an inner restlessness and yearning for something …… something beyond – what?

I dutifully completed my A-levels (as they were called then), took an English degree in Exeter, worked for various publishers in London, got married, and bore two wonderful children. All as it should be. And yet, somewhere trickling beneath the surface, was that constant itch that sneakily scratched and taunted me. A voice that whispered, "You don't belong here. You should be ……." Was it a case of the grass is greener on the other side of the fence?

I have always had a strong sense of duty, and I am intensely loyal – sometimes detrimentally so. Also, though people generally consider me fearless, that is not the case. I am frequently full of doubts and can get my feet firmly jammed in concrete.

My husband and I eventually separated and then divorced, I moved out of London to the border between Dorset and Wiltshire, and my children went to university and left home.

I made some good friends in the village, ran my own small aromatherapy massage business and life was good.

Then what happens? I wake up one morning with an urge so strong that I know I

Simply have to do something about it. I need to leave England and work abroad. And soon. Or it will be too late. Crazy? Maybe. But this time I listened to that persistent voice and acted on it.

I applied for a TEFL (teaching English as a foreign language) course in Lisbon. Why Lisbon? I don't know, except that it was a foreign country and maybe a step in the right direction.

It was an extremely intensive course, as courses often are these days, and when I returned to my Wiltshire village a month later with a teaching certificate, I sank into a state of lethargy. I froze. My feet stuck in concrete.

Looking at myself in the mirror one morning, I shouted, "What are you doing, you coward? You wanted an adventure, didn't you? Then look for one!"

I watched my half-dead eyes begin to brighten. I felt a little flame lick in my innards. I leapt down the stairs to my workroom and started to search for EFL companies who owned schools overseas and started to apply for jobs. A company based in London invited me up for interview. They told me that available posts were thin on the ground as it was early November and most jobs had been taken.

There were, however, still some positions in the Czech Republic, Poland and Russia. I was shown a large map on the wall, with coloured pins where posts were vacant. My mind went blank, until I noted one yellow pin which seemed close to the Republic of Georgia. "Ah ha!" I thought. "My penfriend Marina lives in Tbilisi. I could visit her in the school holiday and get to know her." (On such slim hooks are momentous decisions made!) "I'll take that one," I said, pointing to the yellow pin, and I peered closer at the map. The pin was stuck into a town named Taganrog, which I had never heard of. "They'll be delighted," said the Language Link lady. "They've been waiting for an English teacher for more than three months."

There followed three incredibly hectic weeks. I had to clear my house for tenants, put my personal affairs in order, find temporary homes for my beloved dog and cat, get necessary vaccinations, and prepare my family for my exodus. This was probably just as well. I simply didn't have time to allow my over-fertile imagination to run riot and find all sorts of cogent reasons why I couldn't\shouldn't leave a beautiful, serene corner of Wiltshire.

In every spare moment – there weren't many of those – I mugged up the Russian alphabet and bought a huge Russian dictionary and a considerably smaller Russian grammar. I knew precisely four words in Russian: those for yes, no, thank you and goodbye! I also bought the Lonely Planet Guide to Russia, which warned me that there were all sorts of day-to-day commodities which were difficult, if not impossible, to find anywhere in Russia.

As Taganrog was clearly not a particularly large or important town I decided to play safe and take as many useful teaching aids as I could: collections of poetry and short stories; books with lots of useful illustrations and – a last-minute brainwave which later proved to be invaluable – a six-month postal delivery of the Guardian weekly overseas newspaper.

It was November 1996. Suddenly, with no time to draw breath, it was D-Day, and I was being driven to Heathrow Airport by a kind friend, whose boot was laden with an appalling amount of luggage. Generally, I prefer to travel light, but all those books I might need took up a lot of space and weight.

I was somewhat thrown at Heathrow to be faced with overweight charges of £186 – though given that I'd packed a considerable library I suppose I should have expected it. I knew perfectly well that there was practically nothing in my account until tenants were found for my home, and I breathed a sigh of relief for Access. My heart was pounding and I felt weak with anxiety. Once on the plane, however, I took a deep breath and relaxed. It was too late for regrets. "Russia, here I come!"

MAP OF MY ADVENTURE IN
SOUTHWEST RUSSIA

2 Arrival

I was met at Moscow Airport by a charming company driver called Sasha, who was polite enough not to comment on my amount, and weight, of luggage. He drove me to the Language Link office in central Moscow, where I was to receive a few hours of training before flying on to Rostov on Don.

Natasha, the Director of Studies there, said an odd thing to me: "Gilli, I think you're going to love Russia. But you'll find it very difficult to explain this to your family and friends back home." It was only much later that I understood what she meant.

The plane to Rostov was due to depart at 11.00 p.m. Nice Sasha drove me across Moscow to Vnukovo Airport, where I was charged yet more for overweight luggage, though Sasha tried to persuade the Aeroflot officials that one charge was quite sufficient! Unfortunately, books do weigh a lot.

All us passengers had to wait on the runway because a cleaner hadn't finished her work. She was a large woman in a headscarf and baggy dungarees, who was ineffectively sweeping with a twig broom.

She then waddled down the steps bearing a large black rubbish bag, the contents of which were tossed over our heads onto the concrete.

The plane looked rather kronky. It was packed, and the seats were so close together that I doubted that a large or long-legged person would be able to fit in. Fortunately, I am very small. The flight to Rostov was supposed to take about an hour. I slept fitfully, and was awoken by an incomprehensible announcement shortly before we landed. Glancing at my watch, I noticed that we were late.

The airport was rather primitive, and I was surprised that there was no passport control or checks of any kind. Indeed, there was no sign of any airport officials. All the passengers waited outside in a large open courtyard for about half an hour, after which we trailed into a bleak hall with an antiquated luggage conveyer.

A few tatty boxes and beaten-up bags jiggled along the belt and were claimed by passengers who promptly disappeared. In no time, I found myself entirely alone – with no luggage.

I waited for a while, with fading hope, and then shuffled back out into the courtyard.

There was no sign of anyone waiting for me: I had been told that the school director would pick me up from the airport. Oddly, I didn't feel panicked, I just felt angry about my luggage. I'd paid enough for it to get this far, after all.

I looked at my watch. It was well after midnight. There was a group of men – rather rough looking - standing by a small sort of kiosk so I approached them and asked where were my '*tree bagazhes*'. They were very talkative and waved their arms about a good deal and of course I didn't understand anything!

I kept repeating, with obstinate insistence, that I wanted my luggage. Eventually, three of the men shrugged, gave me looks of pity, and commandeered an open truck, which they drove onto the runway and towards the abandoned Aeroflot plane. They returned with my three cases and plonked them down beside me.

By now it was after 1.00 a.m. I decided it was too late to try phoning the number I'd been given and, anyway, I couldn't see any phones. Perhaps it would be best to just sit the night out in the courtyard and wait till daylight. I think I was too tired and confused to make much sense. I pulled my woollen hat down over my ears, wound my scarf round my neck, snuck as far into my scruffy second-hand sheepskin coat as I could, climbed onto my tower of luggage with my short legs dangling, sighed deeply, and tried to sleep.

After a while, however, I was approached by two of the men by the kiosk, who had a smart woman in a fur coat and hat in tow.

It transpired that she spoke a little English. She explained that – due to fog – the plane had been diverted from Rostov to Krasnodar, wherever that was. I asked her when/whether the plane would continue its journey to Rostov. There ensued a lively discussion on this topic, the general consensus apparently being that, well, it might go tomorrow, or the next day, or not at all. It depended.

Using the lady as a translator, one of the men asked me where I wanted to go. I told him Taganrog, and he offered to drive me there for 300 US dollars. I had only a vague notion of the value of roubles as against dollars, but it sounded very expensive and I was pretty sure I didn't have enough money, so I declined. He was persistent, I was extremely cold, and eventually we agreed on a fee of 200 dollars.

I thanked the woman and followed the man to a very battered car in the 1960s style.

There were what looked like five bullet holes in the windscreen. I gratefully climbed into the back seat while the driver loaded my cases into his boot.

To my surprise, two large men in thick coats climbed into the back – one on either side of me, and a third took the passenger seat. With the driver, that made five of us.

I briefly wondered whether I was going to be kidnapped and ransomed, but so much humanity in such a confined space was already creating warmth so I snuggled back and closed my eyes.

We drove through the night and I slept on and off.

The road was generally very straight and often, I think, raised above the surrounding land, though it was difficult to be sure on account of the thick fog. The driver had a tendency to drive cheerfully on both the left and right sides and approaching headlights would loom out of the darkness in what seemed to me from any direction. But I was honestly past caring and had surrendered my life into the hands of God.

We drove into Taganrog at about 7.00 a.m. The Moscow office had given me the address of my landlady and I passed the information on to the driver. He clearly didn't know the town, and kept stopping to ask people the way.

He eventually found the correct street – Rosa Luxemburg – and I walked rather stiffly to a tall gate in a wall and rang the bell. The gate was opened by a very thin, even gaunt, woman wearing the most extraordinary outfit over wrinkled black stockings and flattened sort of slippers.

I explained who I was. She threw her arms in the air, embraced me, called me "my seester", and ushered me across a courtyard into a house.

She told me that her name was Olga, and then proceeded to make several very long phone calls. Meanwhile, the taxi driver – who had followed us in with the luggage – paced restlessly up and down, ran fingers through his hair, shrugged at me and grimaced, and indicated in mime that he thought the woman was crazy.

Eventually, two more women arrived. One was called Anya and the second was called Valentina, a beautiful voluble blonde who spoke excellent English. I explained to the latter that I needed to pay the driver but didn't have enough cash in dollars and was there a cash machine where I could obtain some. Anya disappeared and soon returned with the remaining cash, and the driver thankfully departed.

After cups of tea all round, I eventually understood that Olga was my landlady, Anya was director of the school, and Valentina (Valya) was a friend who had offered to help initially as the school director spoke little English.

I also discovered that Krasnodar is over 300 km south of Rostov, which is about 50 km from Taganrog.

3 First Days

My landlady, Olga, and her husband, Vitaly, were both retired doctors, and childless. Their house was quite big, and stacked to the ceiling with furniture, like a depository. My little flat was on the upper floor; it was light, clean and quite pretty, but there was practically no furniture, which struck me as odd considering the clutter downstairs. There was nowhere for me to put books and clothes. It was reached via a steep ladder through a loft-type entrance into the little sitting room, which contained two tables and two upright chairs. Off this were the two weeny bedrooms. For the duration of my stay, I lived out of my suitcase. I shared a small kitchen and a minute shower room and next-door toilet with my hosts.

As I arrived on a Wednesday, I was granted a few days to rest and acclimatise, for which I was grateful. I spent most of this time getting to know my hosts, familiarizing myself with the local area, and mugging up Russian.

It was late November. Snow lay thickly everywhere but the sky was a clear blue and it was sunny.

This part of the town seemed very rural, with wide streets, either side of which were strips of land planted with many different kinds of fruit trees.

Quite a lot of chickens were scratching about and there were loads of stray cats and dogs. Most of the houses were brick bungalows, maybe a century old, with heavy wooden shutters and yards behind high fences which, oddly, were mostly made of iron sheets and not wood. I didn't see any shops, though there were occasional kiosks on the pavements selling bread, cigarettes, sweets and items of that sort. There weren't many cars and most of these were at least twenty years old: it was like a time warp. One of the first things I noticed while walking about was the smell of gas. I later discovered that this was actually cheap gasoline.

A half hour walk in one direction took me to the Azov sea-shore. It was not a pretty beach, as it was littered with broken concrete, bits of twisted metal, lumps of limestone and other detritus, but the sea air was invigorating and I was excited at the prospect of living by a great expanse of water.

On Saturday, a pleasant and rather earnest 20-year-old student called Andrei – who used to lodge with Olga and Vitaly – turned up and offered to take me round the town.

We first visited the house where Anton Chekhov was born. It was a tiny little white cottage, like a dolls' house, and charming. We then walked to the main art gallery, housed in a handsome old building which had seen better days.

We were personally shown round by the pretty curator, who spoke no English and lectured with great enthusiasm for a minimum of ten minutes in front of every painting, many of them not really to my taste. She was clearly so proud of the gallery, however, that I smiled, and nodded and feigned as much interest as possible.

Then a female student arrived – I think Andrei had arranged for her to meet us. She translated the curator's spiel for me and it was all I could do to keep a straight face. Her English wasn't bad, but she didn't know any of the art terminology which – being very similar to French and

Italian – was immediately clear to me. It was all great fun and I felt like a VIP.

We must have spent at least three hours in that small gallery and by the time we left I was limp with hunger.

I started teaching on Monday the 25th November. The school was a twenty-minute walk away.

ANTON CHEKHOV'S HOME

I learned later that, during the day, it was a primary school for disadvantaged children, run by a very nice Jewish Russian called Sergei. It had formerly been a Jewish school, when the town had a large Jewish population. Anya rented two classrooms for the language school on weekday evenings.

The building was shabby but functional. My classroom contained desks and chairs and a smallish green chalkboard. Anya used a corner of Sergei's office.

There were no photocopying facilities, so I had to use a small office business a couple of streets away.

The nice blonde lady called Valentina was there every evening, which was a great support. She was a lecturer at the pedagogical institute during the day, but had very kindly volunteered to help me settle in.

I was to teach three classes for an hour and a half each, with a short preparation period between each class, starting at 4 pm and ending at 9 pm. The first class was for teenagers, and the other two for college and university students and working adults. Each student was supplied with a workbook and I had the accompanying teacher's book, plus all the materials I had brought with me. And was I glad for those!

I was somewhat taken aback, not to say amused, to find that my board chalk was two large chunks of chalk – clearly scooped from a limestone cliff and resembling Neolithic tools! They proved so ineffective that I didn't use the board at all until I was able to locate a shop that sold regular chalk sticks.

All three classes were full and the students seemed friendly and very keen. Not surprising, when one considers how long they had been waiting for a native English teacher. During my final adult class, I heard muffled voices from the other side of the classroom door, which then opened a crack.

I could see a vertical line of half-faces peering at me through the crack, before the door closed.

It transpired that these were adult students who were waiting for the second teacher and were intensely curious to see a real live teacher from England. Apparently, they were amazed that I was so small. One of these faces was Ina, who later became a close friend.

I had a bit of a problem with the students' names. Anya had given me class lists written in Russian cyrillic script. I could read printed letters – upper and lower case – but handwritten letters are formed very differently and I couldn't make head or tail of them. I asked Vitaly to read out the names so that I could transcribe them on my registers, which he obligingly did. However, this list still didn't conform to the names the students themselves told me, so – feeling very stupid – I checked this out with Valentina. Vitaly had given me Christian names plus the patronyms, but what I needed was surnames. Any readers of Russian novels might understand my confusion.

TEENAGE CLASS

For example, Michail Ivanovich (son of Ivan) Pushkin would be addressed formally as Michail Ivanovich (not Mr Pushkin), and by his familiars as Misha. His sister Ekatarina Ivanovna (daughter of Ivan) would be

Ekatarina Ivanovna, or Katya to her familiars. Just to further compound my problem, there doesn't seem to be a great choice of names in Russia (rather like in Wales). In my teenage class of nine, there were three Katyas, and in my late class of fifteen students, there were three Julias and three Alexeis. Andrei and Olga

ADULT CLASS

were other very common names.

I really enjoyed my first day's teaching, and soon overcame my initial nerves. However, on the second evening I had an alarming experience in the final class.

Everything started okay, but as the lesson progressed I began to feel as if my mind was shutting down.

I kept forgetting perfectly common words, so there were awkward silences as I struggled to continue. I battled on until about half an hour before the close, when I just blanked out. My head felt like an empty bowl and I couldn't speak at all. What on earth was I to do? Fighting down panic, I decided that there was nothing for it but to indicate that I had to stop. I pulled up a chair, sat down, and mimed that I couldn't think or speak.

One student, a kind bearded man called Igor, came up to me and 'laid his hands on me', and then began to vigorously whirl his arms very near my face like a demented windmill. I suspect he was trying to give me more air. Some kind person then drove me home.

Thank goodness this happened in the adult class and not with the teens.

I felt no better the next morning. My mind was buzzy and blank; eyelids heavy; no appetite; mild diarrhoea; flaccid and weak.

Olga took my temperature and blood pressure, gave me pills and potions, crooned

"Eat! Eat!" and filled my bed with GLASS bottles filled with boiling water, which rolled around and scorched me. Anya, Valentina and others came in an endless stream to my bedside, arguing as to best treatments, and I felt like a hopeless goldfish in a small bowl. The student Andrei turned up with bottled water and advised me not to drink Olga's water. Then Igor arrived with a very large bottle of pink water together with a leaflet in Russian about all its healing properties. When I had a moment alone with Valentina, I told her I suspected that I was suffering from delayed shock: an awful lot had happened in the past few weeks and this might be the reaction.

The next morning, still feeling rather weak and floppy, I got dressed mid-morning and took a walk to the sea. The weather was cold, but bright and sunny and the sea air did me good. On my return I found Anya in the kitchen and told her I would return to work on Friday. Everyone clucked but I was adamant.

I felt bad enough as it was, letting everyone down, and I was determined to develop a regular routine as soon as possible.

4 Paul

While I was still in England, Language Link had informed me that they had contracted another teacher, Paul, who would be joining me some time in December. I had phoned him to introduce myself and we had had a pleasant chat. I was relieved to learn that he had lived in Russia for a while and spoke reasonable Russian.

Shortly after my collapse, Anya took the train to Moscow to collect Paul. She had told me that Paul was apparently VERY LARGE and I wondered how he would fit into the tiny bathroom.

Two days later she arrived at the flat with Valentina in tow to tell me that Paul "had vanished". She had put him on a train to Rostov (I couldn't quite understand why she didn't accompany him) and he hadn't been seen or heard of since.

Every day there were long, loud phone calls, and women came and went, flapping and clucking.

Vitaly and I found it rather wearing, and kept escaping into the yard for a bit of peace and quiet.

On the Friday of that week, 6th December, the phone rang soon after I got back from school. It was a very poor line and the phone was passed from hand to hand as we tried to make it out. It was definitely a man and I suggested that it could be Paul as I remembered he had a deep voice and the rhythm of speech sounded English to me.

So, in hope, Anya drove to Rostov station. It was indeed Paul. He arrived, looking exhausted and very large, at about 1.30 a.m.

Apparently his train went via the Ukraine and, as he didn't have a Ukrainian visa, he was removed from the train by police, spent several hours in the local police station, and then was put on a train returning to Russia. He went to a place called Oryol, where he spent the best part of a day, and then was shunted to and fro, before eventually getting a connection to Rostov.

Paul seemed very nice – tolerant, warm and easy-going. And despite his ghastly experience he was able to see the funny side of things. He raised his eyebrows laconically when he saw that the entrance to our flat via the attic ladder was barely large enough for him to ease through, and grunted with laughter when I showed him the minute bathroom.

The bath, which was short anyway, was stacked with mirrors and other paraphernalia at one end, so you had to ease yourself into the shower end and keep your elbows well in. Nor was he troubled by the fact that there was nowhere to hang his clothes. Mind you, he wasn't exactly sartorial and I doubted that clothes and tidiness were of much importance to him.

Having lived in Russia before, Paul was in a good position to put me straight on certain points: for instance, in relation to our landlord and landlady. Although Olga and Vitaly had what I considered to be some strange routines, I had assumed – in my innocence – that this was normal in southwest Russia. For example, they never – as far as I could see – ate together.

Indeed, Olga didn't seem to eat much at all, but when she did, she ate alone or shared some cake with me. Vitaly kept a small saucepan on a hook screwed to the outside kitchen wall. In this he boiled potatoes and ate them straight out of the pan; he chewed raw garlic cloves and drank a soupy sour yoghurt called kefir out of a glass jar. He always ate standing up, usually out in the yard. Indeed, he never appeared to sit down at all. The only time I had seen him do so was when he visited me in the flat when Olga was out. The couple rarely spoke to one another, and yet I never heard them arguing.

When I expressed my puzzlement to Paul he laughed outright. "Gilli dear," he said, "Olga is as nutty as a fruit cake. The house and money are hers; he hasn't got a bean. She treats him like a serf." Vitaly was extremely intelligent and, despite my poor Russian and his scant English, we had managed to communicate pretty well. I now realised that his quiet tolerance and odd habits were due to an independent spirit and personal pride. If Olga didn't want to share her wealth and possessions with him, then he would manage without. He was often out of the house, and I discovered that he spent many hours in the local telegraph office, from where I made the occasional call to my family. The building was well heated and had benches all along the wall. Vitaly would sit there and read for hours. He always took an easel along with him, on which was propped a rather good cartoon-style painting done by him. I guessed that this painting was there to kind of justify his regular presence. Occasionally, someone would ask him whether the painting was for sale, but he never sold it! Paul and I would often pop into the telegraph office to sit and talk to him.

Sometimes, when Olga was out, Vitaly would ascend our ladder and join us for a chat. On one such occasion, I noticed that both his wrists, though clearly strong, were crooked, and I asked him about this.

He told me that many years before, in winter, he and the ambulance driver were speeding to an emergency in an isolated homestead. The road, as often in these parts, was a narrow one raised above the surrounding flat land, so when the ambulance suddenly skidded on black ice, it shot off the road and landed upside down. Though injured, Vitaly and his co-worker managed to right the vehicle and get it up on the road, and they continued to their destination. They gave emergency treatment to the patient and drove him to the nearest hospital where, later, Vitaly was also examined. He had broken both his wrists! This courageous man was in no way boasting. He was simply telling it as it was. All in a day's work.

5 TAGANROG TOWN AND PEOPLE

It's not really surprising that I had never heard of Taganrog before I came to Russia. The Russian Lonely Planet Guide grants it four short paragraphs on account of two points of possible interest to travellers. Peter the Great planned to make it an important naval base, as Turkey was a thorn in his side, but no sooner had work started on a large fort than the problems with the Turks came to an end, and his political interests veered northward to the Baltic Region. He therefore leaped on his white charger and galloped north, to found a splendid city on marshland by the Baltic Sea – St Petersburg – leaving Taganrog to 'stew in its own juice'. Its second claim to fame is that Anton Chekhov grew up there; his family moved away when he was nineteen.

Another possible reason why it is not much known is that it was one of Russia's closed towns (i.e. closed to foreigners) for many years on account of its huge military aircraft factory. There is still an aircraft plant, but it is a shadow of its former self.

At one time, in true Soviet tradition, the plant was a mini-city, comprising workers' housing, sports and art centres, schools, hospitals and sanatoriums, holiday camps and rural areas where the workers could acquire a bit of land and grow their own food. These thousands of workers certainly had special privileges.

In addition to constructing aeroplanes, the workers of Taganrog are employed in the manufacture of industrial pipes and in iron and steel production in a big way. As there's not much woodland in the area, metal is used in place of wood: many garden 'fences' are sheets of iron, as are ping pong tables! Judging by my students, the other vocational draws to citizens of the USSR are a large Pedagogical Institute (for training teachers) and the Radiotechnical University. Many of my students were either training to be teachers or computer programmers. These students came from all corners of the old Soviet Union: Siberia, Tashkent, Sakhalin Island, the Caucasus, Novorossirsk; from Azerbaijan, Armenia, the Ukraine and elsewhere.

Geographically, Taganrog is in the Rostov Region, Rostov-on-Don being the nearest big city.

This region is criss-crossed with many rivers and is generally pretty flat, though moving water has gouged out a lot of gullies which are not obvious until one stumbles on one. There are not many big trees, but huge fields full of beautiful wild flowers wherever crops are not planted, and reed beds galore.

A TAGANROG STREET

Surrounded by very fertile soil – the sediment of the Don and Miusky estuaries - it has a distinctly agricultural feel about it.

Many of the residential streets are lined with fruit trees and green verges and fruit and vegetables in the markets are fresh, cheap and of excellent quality. Being only five kilometres from the East Ukrainian border, the town also benefits from the produce of Ukrainian smallholders who come into the town in droves every weekend.

Taganrog is on a peninsula sticking out into the eastern Azov Sea, which is not salty at this point and is almost more like a large lake adjoined to the Black Sea.

The town is raised above the water on crumbly chalk cliffs, and I saw many instances of buildings teetering over the edge. Apparently there were many more beach facilities until some freak high tides destroyed most of these and they had not generally been replaced during the time I lived there. Some of the beaches were littered with lumps of concrete and other materials. Nor were there many tourists – certainly no foreign ones – or holiday hotels.

There was a small working port below the remnants of Peter the Great's fort. Any bulky cargo ships had to moor on floating piers some way out to sea as the sea was shallow and the shipping lanes frequently silted up. While I was working in Taganrog, I heard there were plans to update and greatly enlarge the port, but at the time I doubted this would happen. It would be an extremely costly enterprise and would require constant upkeep and dredging. Mind you, with the loss of the Black Sea ports on the Ukraine, the only Russian port in the area, apart from little Taganrog, was Novorossirsk.

According to my glossy town map and local guide, Taganrog had a population of 450,000 souls – a small town by Russian standards. It boasted 12 restaurants, 16 hotels, 2 nightclubs and 1 theatre. I have a problem with this information, although it was a fact that the local people did not actually eat out much. There were apparently 40 primary schools, all of which had two shifts of six hours each: the first from 7.00 am to 1.00, and the second from 1.00 to 6.00. It took me a considerable while to come to grips with various aspects of the town. For instance, I was puzzled that there seemed to be hardly any actual shops for a town of its size.

A TAGANROG BEACH

Yes, there were numerous little kiosks on the pavements, many of which stayed open all night.

If you needed something and no one was in evidence, you knocked on the glass and eventually a sleepy kiosk keeper would rise up from an invisible bed to serve you. But most of these sold sweets, ice creams, cigarettes and bread.

One Saturday, as I was strolling around to see what I could see, and learn what I could learn (this was before Paul arrived), I turned a corner and saw a queue of people outside a large wooden door. Curiosity prompted me to join the line. It took me an interminable time to see what was inside, which puzzled me initially, until I realised that the old women (for they formed the majority) were dab hands at barging through the line without appearing to do so, with the result that I remained at the back.

When I did eventually enter the building, which was concrete and abysmally dark and drear, I found that I was in a dairy, selling very fresh and excellent milk products of all kinds. After this experience, I regularly tagged onto queues, and in most instances they led me to an interesting shop. The reason I hadn't spotted them was that the windows were generally barred and blind, or filthy, and there were no signs of any sort outside. Clearly, Taganrogians did not go in for advertising and display.

There were many open markets and, being a lover of markets, I did almost all my shopping in one or other of these. You could find everything there in time. There were old women selling jars of delicious homemade yoghurt, pickles, fresh tomato juice, dried beans, dried flowers, herbs for cooking and to be used as remedies.

Great stone slabs were piled high with meat, poultry and an enormous variety of fish. There were sacks of flour, rice, lentils, semolina; vats of sauerkraut; churns and jars of milk, curds and whey, and many varieties of soured milk, cream and yoghurt. One lovely lady I regularly visited had a great mound of delicious halva on a board, and would slice you off a great chunk. As well as huge piles of fruit and vegetables, there were little clumps of this 'n that carefully arranged on a piece of cloth or paper on the ground– the pickings from small allotments. Then there was the Korean contingent with their ready-made spicy vegetables and fish salads. In addition to all the food, there was hardware, clothes, spare parts for absolutely everything. Sadly, there were also the beggars, usually still and quiet, waiting patiently for the odd kopek. And lurking everywhere, stray cats and dogs on the make – usually pretty successfully.

Public phone boxes were plentiful, and extremely cheap to use, but the sound quality was so poor that they were as good as useless. Public transport was also very cheap and you rarely had to wait long for a tram or bus, though they were generally crowded. Taxis were reasonable too.

Apparently there used to be a sizeable Greek population and quite a few of my students had Greek blood. There was also at one time a large number of Jews. Looking at the position of Taganrog on a map, one can see that it is more than likely that many different peoples would have travelled through these parts and some of them would have stayed and gone no further. (See Neal Ascherson's The Black Sea, Vintage 1996, for a full history of this area.)

There were certainly many different physical types – Slavik, Mongolian, Tatar, Turkik – and there were the Cossacks. Indeed, so important were the Cossacks in this region, that they deserve a chapter to themselves (see chapter 6).

The Slavic population are generally tall and very good looking, with beautiful eyes, high and rather flat cheekbones and full-lipped mouths. The men all look incredibly young, until they get to about fifty when they often age very quickly. I learned to be careful, on early acquaintance, about the sort of questions I asked.

I had been caught out with apparently innocuous questions such as: "Which school do you go to?" to which the answer was, "Well.

I'm an engineer, married, with two children." The only other places where I've seen so many beautiful women is in Tuscany and Bali. It was very rare to see a teenage girl who was dumpy, plain and spotty. The younger women only sported two blemishes. Their teeth were often poor – I suspect on account of the local water – and gum infections could lead to bad breath. Also, they often had deformed feet on account of the cheap high-heeled shoes they wore. The women generally took great care with their appearance, which is not surprising given the dowdiness of available clothes during the years of communism. However straitened their circumstances, they would have their hair done regularly, make up every day, and dress smartly.

My friend Galya visited England for the first time and liked the country, but she was shocked at how little trouble most women took with their appearance. She couldn't understand it at all and it rather upset her.

Many of the townspeople thought nothing of hawking and spitting in public, but were horrified if one used a tissue to blow one's nose. I remember sitting on a tram with Paul when I had a streaming cold. I pulled a tissue from my coat pocket and blew my nose vigorously, and then realised that Paul was choking with laughter. "What's the joke?" I asked. "Did you see the expressions of the people opposite?" he cackled. "They were absolutely disgusted and tried to move away." I hadn't noticed as it happened, mainly because the tissue (a Russian one, of course) had disintegrated following the first blow and I had been desperately trying to catch the wafting feathers of paper before they landed on someone's knee.

Another thing that intrigued me was the locals' attitude to noise. I don't mean the sound of traffic or the pretty constant banging noises from the iron and steel plant, but people noise.

One experience comes to mind. On one of my regular tram journeys two women, who were almost certainly drunk, started to fight.

They were staggering up and down the aisle, screaming blue murder, pulling out chunks of hair, tearing one another's clothes and punching each other in the face. No one appeared to take much notice of them, and certainly nobody tried to separate them, but eventually several elderly women berated the two hell cats for 'making so much noise'. In other words, kill one another if you must, but do it quietly.

As I got to know people better and visited them in their homes, I realised that most lived in tiny (often one-bedroom) flats in large residential blocks where one's neighbours' noise easily percolated through the walls and ceilings. This could well explain their attitude to 'people noise'. In general, I did find Russians tended to speak quietly.

The few Russians I got to know early on were very kind and hospitable, and invited me to their homes for meals. I was a little worried that I was bringing them the wrong sort of gifts – flowers, or chocolates, or a bottle of wine - as they never thanked me. I asked Valya (Valentina) about this and she assured me that my gifts were very welcome However, it was not generally considered polite to open a present in front of the giver or to refer to it in any way, as the host should concentrate solely on the comfort of the visitor. Also, if presenting flowers, one should ensure that they were an odd number – counted by the stems, not the flowers – as even-numbered stems were only used for funerals.

Russian timekeeping seemed odd too. Many shops, offices, the post office, closed for lunch, but the meal seemed to be a moveable feast – any time between midday and 4.30 pm!

I heard it said that in the big factories, which all have their own canteens, the canteen workers took time off at the same time as the workers. I decided that this was probably a myth as the Russians do like laughing at themselves.

When living in a foreign country, one will inevitably find some aspects rather strange, but human beings are human beings, whatever their culture, and ultimately we are all the same, the differences being only skin deep. That is something I have discovered in my travels and I believe the world would be a much happier place if we all understood this. We could then happily respect, and even enjoy, the cultural differences, which provide colour and variety, whilst comfortably connecting with other peoples at a deeper level of common humanity.

6 THE COSSACKS

I knew that the Taganrog area was a Cossack region, and I also knew that Cossacks had a reputation for being fierce warriors and great horsemen. As I love horses and horse riding, I was looking forward to having opportunities to ride regularly. I was disappointed. There were very few horses in the area. I learned that vast numbers of horses died in the First World War and the Russian Revolution, and many of those that survived were eaten during the terrible years of starvation. Also, once horses were no longer needed for transport and agriculture, they became a luxury that few people could afford.

Taganrog was very proud of its Cossack credentials, and the town of Novocherkassk, about two hours' drive away, was the capital of the southern Cossacks. But I was puzzled as to who, exactly, these people were. Were they Slavs, with the flat, high cheekbones and full lips; or were they perhaps the tall, thin people with thin, sharp features and pointed noses that I saw around Taganrog?

Eventually, I discovered that the Cossacks were not in fact a race at all. They were actually escaped serfs and other independent-minded adventurers who broke away from the more settled regions to the north – mainly in Muscovy and Poland – and formed small military-style bands that robbed travellers and plundered trading vessels plying the big rivers such as the Volga and the Don.

By the early seventeenth century, some of these nomadic freebooters had formed more settled communities, occupying the mainly uninhabited swathes of steppe land to the south-east and south of Moscow. Some travelled still further south, to the unpopulated region of rolling grassland and great rivers known as 'Wild Fields'. They took wives, farmed the land, hunted and fished. They had no particular political allegiance – though the ex-Muskovites were often fiercely orthodox – valued their independence, and elected their own chiefs (atmans). Cossacks were often a thorn in the sides of the ruling autocrats but could, if persuaded and rewarded, be useful in the role of auxiliaries. Indeed, various tsars partially solved the Cossack problem by negotiating with the atmans.

In return for annual government subsidies, tax allowances, and the right to hold their land and administrate their own territories, the Cossacks agreed to supply auxiliary units when required. These soldiers supplied their own horses, tackle, weapons and uniforms, and were supposed to attend training camps for a minimum of three weeks per year.

The more northerly Cossacks formed several regiments loyal to the tsar and were, indeed, the crème de la crème of the tsarist forces. The Cossack communities of the south, however, in the Rostov Region, the Kuban (just north of the Caucasus) and the Ukraine, preferred their independence and were generally farmers and merchants.

Because the Cossacks were such gritty fighters, they were often sent to the hot trouble spots and, when roused, they could exert considerable influence on the outcomes. For instance, in 1613 the Cossack support for 16-year-old Mikhail Romanov as the new tsar was crucial.

In 1670, a rebellion was led by a Don Cossack chieftain called Razin. Though the main grievance was the abolition of a government subsidy, Razin sympathised with the plight of the serfs, who were mere chattels with no rights. The rebels were defeated by the tsar's superior forces, but Razin is still celebrated in song and myth.

In the eighteenth century, under the iron rules of Peter the Great and Catherine II, the Russian empire extended south into the vast area of the Ukraine, Crimea and the Don region, all the way to the Caucasus. Though generally pro-tsarist, the Don Cossacks resented this interference and rebelled. Punishment was swift and severe: about 14,000 men, women and children were slaughtered.

During the Russian Revolution the Don Cossacks generally supported the White Russians, but there were enough who sided with the Reds to cause tragic splits in many families. Mikhail Sholokhov's 2-volume novel, Quiet Flows the Don and The Don Flows Home to the Sea give a colourful and moving account of these times.

The southern Cossacks are traditionally represented in two, very different, ways. In one scenario, they are passionate about their land, their homes, their families, and there are many songs that celebrate this passion. In the other view, they are fierce and ruthless fighters, feared and hated by those peoples who fear them, rough and barbarous.

I personally came to know several Cossack families who could not have been kinder and more hospitable, and who were cultured and open-minded.

7 Hospital

My students told me that the twelfth December was a public holiday – New Constitution Day. I asked them what constitution the day was intended to celebrate. They all shrugged, and one student replied: "Our government make a new constitution every year. We do not know what constitution. We just celebrate!" I got the impression that Russians were even more sceptical about their governments than the British were, and probably with good reason.

Not long after this, my students began falling off. I was a bit worried that maybe it was due to my teaching, but Anya assured me that this was due to 'winter illnesses'. Not surprisingly, I, too, eventually succumbed to what I took to be the local 'flu'.

After over a week of bedrest and homeopathic remedies, plus my own aromatherapy inhalations, I felt no better.

One evening I decided there was nothing for it but to attempt to live life again. I dragged myself out of bed, laboriously descended the ladder, and shuffled along the corridor to the kitchen, at which point I blacked out. I came to, lying face down on the kitchen floor. A pair of large, gentle hands felt my pulse, lifted me onto a stool, and laid my head on a folded cloth on the table.

Vitaly, for it was he, managed to carry me up that ladder and tuck me into bed. A doctor arrived a little later and gave me more medicine, but two days later I developed severe bronchitic symptoms and it was decided that I should be taken to hospital. I have a dread of hospitals, almost certainly as a result of experiences in childhood, but was too weak to resist.

I was hospitalised for about a week, all through Christmas. I was given drips every alternate day, and bum injections on the days between, and had to swallow a great many bright blue and red pills. My room was bare, dreary and none too clean; there was no water during the day in the bathroom; and the food was unbelievably dreadful. I shared the room with a rather charming mouse that would scamper out from under the fridge at night. I'm ashamed to say that I was not a good patient. I was surly and suspicious and sometimes refused to undergo any more injections.

Valya was a regular visitor and gave me a talking-to, which had a positive effect! She, Anya, and several students visited me from time to time, bringing fresh fruit, bread, jars of bottled fruit and vegetables, for which I was immensely grateful.

Someone also brought me a 'kettle', which consisted of an element dangling on the end of a flex. You plugged it into a wall socket and dropped the element into a glass jar of water and, hey presto, you had boiling water to brew tea and coffee.

On the evening of Christmas Day, Valya turned up with her husband Genio, whom I hadn't met before. They brought a bottle of champagne, glasses, chocolates and other nibbles, and stayed for a couple of hours. I forgot my troubles in the joy of celebrating with two such splendid people: so much kindness, determination and integrity.

The hospital general facilities may have been dire, but the staff were excellent and, whatever treatments they handed out to me, they worked. I paid a last visit to the specialist– a delightful man called Dr Nikolai Nikolaevich – on the 29th December, my fiftieth birthday, and walked out of the hospital into a cold, crisp day with a brilliant blue sky and thick snow. I stopped in a market on the way home to buy alcohol and special food as I was determined to celebrate my birthday in style.

I hunted for a bottle of good champagne and eventually located one on a small stall. As it appeared to be the only one, I placed it on the ground between my feet as I rummaged in my rucksack for my wallet.

Suddenly, I was attacked by the blonde stallholder, who pulled my woolly hat and hair and shrieked at me. I tried to explain that I was looking for my money as she clearly thought I was planning to steal the bottle. Then her husband joined forces with her, and he kicked me! Feeling shaken and extremely indignant, I wobbily heaved myself upright, swore at them roundly in English, and marched off without the champagne.

Well, that was the intention, but I slipped on sheet ice, flew into the air, and landed bottom first on the next-door stall, sending products flying in all directions.

By this time, everybody seemed to be yelling at me. I decided to make an exit with as much dignity as possible – which was precious little!

However, I still managed to cook a very nice dinner for myself and Paul, which made me feel better.

With hindsight, I realise how much my condition was of concern, both to Russian colleagues and friends and to my wretched family in the UK, who were apparently on the point of flying to Russia to drag me home. I suspect, too, that my condition must have cost the school a good deal of money, as medical treatment doesn't come free in Russia, and yet I was not asked to pay a rouble. When all's said and done, I was very well cared for by everyone involved, and I owe them a sackful of thanks.

In Russia, New Year is more important to most people than Christmas, which tends to be a quiet family time, with or without church attendance, and there is no public holiday either.

I gave Olga my landlady some fragrant skin cream and Vitaly a simple English puzzlebook with crosswords and other fun activities, which delighted him.

Paul and I had been invited to Valya and Genio's for New Year. We arrived terribly late because we couldn't find the correct block (my fault!), but fortunately we bumped into Genio being dragged across the yard by their huge black dog, Geoffrey, and arrived just in time to raise our glasses to the new year. We met their beautiful teenage daughters, Maria and Anna, and some neighbours. There was a tremendous feast and enough alcohol to sink the Titanic.

When we finally left in the early hours, I expressed a childish desire to go tobogganing. The night was cold and starry and the snow sparkled delightfully in the dim street lights. Genio and Valya walked partway home with us, drawing their sledge. We swooped down a short incline, first singly and then in pairs, and pushed each other along the tram tracks. Genio lobbed a firecracker against the side of a concrete residential block. The explosion reverberated in the clear icy air, making one's blood tingle with excitement.

It left a sinister black smudge high up on the wall. It was an excellent evening.

8 Moscow

As there was a two-week holiday over Christmas and New Year, Paul and I had decided to explore Moscow. Language Link had told us that several of their teachers' flats would be vacated at this time and they would arrange for us to use one of them.

On the day of departure, snow was lying thickly everywhere and no trams were running. I was afraid the trains might be cancelled too, but thankfully there was no problem there.

The electric train from Taganrog was very handsome with dark green carriages and a bright green and orange striped engine. It wasn't so smart within, however. There was no heating and the bitter wind whooshed through the wooden floorboards. Despite the cold, I enjoyed the nearly two-hour journey to Rostov. We followed the course of a frozen river and saw quite a lot of men and boys fishing through holes drilled in the ice.

Rostov station was large, dreary and freezing. There were some feeble attempts at Christmas decorations: occasional tatty lengths of tinsel wound round a pillar and, on a newspaper stand, a large card showing Father Christmas lying ecstatically on his back, apparently being raped by two curvaceous naked angels.

I saw an old man with crutches lying on the cold stone floor. A bearded Russian came over to him, tenderly lifted the one-legged cripple, laced his one boot, braided his trailing empty trouser leg, and carefully led him to a seat. The price of the electric train was equivalent to 80 pence, while the return ticket to Moscow (about 1,000 km each way) was about £65, and the journey would take 23 hours. The Moscow train was called the 'Tikki Don' (Quiet Don) and had at least twenty carriages and a huge diesel engine. Our sleeping compartment contained four berths and a small table. We were given two laundered sheets, a pillow case and a small hand towel each and there were folded blankets on the bunks. At one end of each carriage was the stewardess's couchette, opposite an electric samovar where boiling water was available. On request, she supplied passengers with stakans (glasses in metal bases), cutlery and toilet paper.

At the other end, beyond the toilet, was a small, rather disgusting room for smokers.

A quiet, elderly man shared our compartment. He greeted us, climbed up to his bunk, and never uttered another word.

Our other neighbour boarded the train a couple of hours later at Novocherkassk – the Cossack capital of the Don area. He was resplendent in a tall fur hat, a handsome waisted and skirted suede jacket and tall suede boots. He tossed his small case on the other top bunk, dipped his head to avoid it crunching on the ceiling, shook hands with Paul and me, and introduced himself as Valeri. He was extremely tall and slim, with a shock of brown hair standing up like a brush and laughing gre333y eyes. When he smiled he looked very rakish as he had several gold teeth.

He informed us that he was a Cossack via many generations and worked as a metalwork manager for a big plant. He was going to Moscow to chase up raw materials that had been paid for in early November but had not materialised.

Within ten minutes of arriving, he unpacked a small briefcase and the national raffia blue-striped bag, and spread an amazing feast on the small table:

a whole smoked pike (caught and smoked by himself); homemade pork sausages; jars of mixed salad; hardboiled eggs; black bread; and a vast assortment of alcohol: Amoretti, vodka and samogon (home-brewed alcohol). He nodded at the table and invited Paul and I to dig in.

We talked far into the night and the old man occasionally joined in with a delicate snore.

Our compartment got hotter and hotter, and we slowly peeled off layers of clothing. By the time we sank onto our bunks my head was floating a good foot above my body. I became distantly aware of a soft murmur somewhere near my right ear and then found my hair, neck and shoulders being caressed. Valeri was hunkered on the floor, whispering sweet nothings and trying to remove the remainder of my clothes! Paul was already snoring loudly. Suddenly, the train drew into a well-lit station, the old man opposite sat up, stared blankly at us, and fell back, and I pushed Valeri away and pulled the sheet over me.

I remembered nothing more, until I was rudely awakened by a terrific crash. I struggled to find my light switch and could hear Paul doing likewise in the bunk opposite.

Valeri was lying on the floor face down. He so exactly fitted the narrow space – the crown of his head pressed against the outer wall under the table and the soles of his feet flat against the door– that he resembled a corpse in its coffin. We somehow managed to heave him into a sitting position. I noticed quite a few splodges of blood on the floor so I examined him as best I could. He had a cut on his forehead and another on one hand, but nothing serious. I mopped him up with some bottled water and tissues and improvised a temporary bandage for his hand. He must have hit the table on his way down and had broken two stakans. How Paul and I managed to heave him back onto his bunk I'll never know.

At about 9.00 am, as I was writing up my diary, I heard a slight movement above me, and a moment later two long legs slithered past me to the floor. Valeri greeted me cheerfully and strode off down the corridor, returning a while later with ten bottles of beer! He scooped a home-cured ham (excellent) and more sausages from his bottomless bag and again invited us to join him. Neither Paul nor I touched the beer. Valeri, however, drank steadily throughout the day.

By the time our train drew into Kazan Station in Moscow at 3.00 pm he was almost paralytic.

Paul and I got his minimal luggage sorted out, and then made a fair attempt to get him dressed as he was clad in nothing more than a vest and long johns. Once the train creaked and ground to a halt, we placed a bag in either hand and supported him to the exit. He got down the steep steps to the platform without falling, and I watched him walk away. It was easy to make him out in the crowds as he was a good head taller than everyone else. Amazingly, he loped along the platform as straight as a die, not a trip or a stutter. What a character! That said, the consumption of alcohol in Russia – particularly among men – is a sad and serious problem. Much of it is of very poor quality and I learned, early on, not to touch vodka.

The flat we'd been lent, near the Botanic Gardens, was extremely comfortable, with large well-proportioned rooms, good quality furniture and lovely rugs on the floor. There was also a big-screen television that actually worked, so we were able to treat ourselves to plenty of films in the evenings. As the flat was on the top of a high block, we had excellent views of Moscow too.

I woke to a beautiful peachy dawn. Some great and coal tits were hanging from birch seeds outside the window. Four huge hooded crows were jawing on an untidy nest at my eye level. Paul and I took the metro to the Lubjanka. The Moscow metro is magnificent – like a huge, amazingly cheap museum and art gallery. At that time, it cost one rouble for a token which took you anywhere in the system for a day. In every station one saw ornate marble columns, brilliant stained glass, Byzantine-style mosaics, chunky reliefs of workers in the Communist style and wonderful Art Nouveau lamps and fal-de-rals. It was enchanting. Also, the metro system was much warmer than above ground so it was the natural place to meet up with friends. I would have been happy just travelling from one station to another for hours.

I felt a chill run down my spine as I craned up at the sinister building in the Lubjanka, which must bear the shadow of countless atrocities. From there we walked to Red Square. St Basil's cathedral – famed for its colourful onion domes – was a dream outside but rather disappointing inside. The History Museum was closed for repairs and, sadly, Lenin's Mausoleum was also closed.

There were quite a few hawkers in the square, and one man approached me with a splendid fur hat complete with communist badge (US$15). I could never have brought myself to buy a new fur, but I was extremely cold and liked this old hat very much, so I bought it. It was a bit large for me as it was really a man's hat, and had ear flaps. I later stuffed it with a roll of newspaper and it then fitted me snugly.

We passed the tomb of the unknown soldier with its eternal flame, which I found moving, crossed the Kutabya Bridge alongside the Supreme Soviet Building, and then walked past an enormous cannon and the Tsar Bell. The latter is apparently the biggest bell ever to be forged in Russia. Of course, it cracked badly when firing and a great chunk broke off, so it sits forlornly on the ground and has never been rung. Is biggest always best?

The Kremlin complex is huge and impressive. There are five churches, all covered from floor to ceiling with magnificent frescoes and icons. What surprised me about them was how relatively small they all were inside, and the fact that they had no seats.

Congregations of the Russian Orthodox Church were clearly expected to stand and worship. Mind you, it was perfectly acceptable to wander in and out during a service.

Towards evening, the central Kremlin square filled up with an enormous crowd, and there was a march past of literally thousands of children, each child carrying an identical bright orange plastic lunch box.

Paul and I concluded that it must be a special New Year Children's Day for children from the outlying provinces. The next day we decided to take a look at the Bolshoi Theatre, which is aptly named as it is very large. It was elegant in a soft apricot stone with soaring pillars and four rearing bronze horses above the entrance. There was a tall Christmas tree in front, decorated – on closer inspection – with large round plaques surrounded with little lights advertising Maggi Soups! I later learned that the previous mayor of Moscow had announced that it was shameful that their capital city was so drab during the Christmas season.

He issued a proclamation that all shops and public places had to decorate their premises or they would risk losing their trading licences. This explained the number of shops I saw displaying about six inches of tatty tinsel pinned or scotch-taped to the entranceway. No doubt the Bolshoi did a deal with the Maggi Company in return for some advertising!

The following morning we visited the Tretyakov Gallery, which housed a splendid family collection of Russian paintings. As with many Russian museums, after buying our tickets we had to put on terrible felt slippers, that looked like squashed kippers, over our shoes to protect the polished floors.

I next hunted vainly for somewhere to cash some travellers' cheques as I owed Paul a considerable amount. I eventually found a cash point that was open, walked in, and was promptly marched out again by a fierce guard carrying a gun.

Paul hooted with laughter and commented: "Trust you to ignore the queue!"

Only then did I realise that the long line of people I had passed in the street were all waiting to get money, added to which there was a large notice outside the entrance stating 'Only one person at a time'. So I had a long wait in -12^0C until my turn, only to be informed that they didn't cash travellers' cheques. By this time we were both weak with hunger. Rather unusually for Moscow, we hadn't seen any cafes or restaurants in the area but there was apparently a McDonalds in the vicinity. I'm not a fan of burgers or chips, but hunger won the day. The building was vast and absolutely packed.

There were horrendous queues at every counter. Still, it was warm in there and I enjoyed reading Big Mac in Russian. Never had a double Mac and cheese tasted so delicious! We then raced through thickly falling snow to the Bolshoi, arriving with few minutes to spare.

We shared our box with a fat, slobby American businessman who had a silent Russian woman in tow, and a little elderly Russian lady who stood for almost the entire performance, despite there being several vacant seats. I don't know why, but I had the feeling that she attended performances pretty regularly.

I was told that Russian citizens could buy an opera ticket for about 6000 roubles (just over US$1). The American and his girl left after the first act, which was a relief as he ate crunchy nibbles non-stop and made loud inane comments at regular intervals. I thoroughly enjoyed La Traviata, despite scenery that had seen better days and poor lighting.

On Monday, our last day in Moscow, it was still snowing and the thermometer in the flat read -17^{0}C. I managed to cash some cheques at last, and we reached Kazan Station with half an hour to spare. Our companions in the couchette were an Armenian couple, Zhore and Vika. He was a businessman and she a Russian teacher. He was small and strong with curly black hair, a splendid moustache and a mouthful of gold teeth. She was small and

BOLSHOI THEATRE CHRISTMAS TREE WITH
MAGGI SOUPS ADVERT DECORATIONS

plump with dyed blonde hair, blue eyes, blood-red nails and lips, and a soft, sexy voice.

After preliminary greetings, they told us they had a grown family in Chechnya and then sat quietly and rather primly opposite us. I murmured to Paul that I thought we'd have a peaceful return journey, to which he replied huskily, "Ho, ho!" I don't know how he knew!

Within ten minutes of departure, they unloaded vast quantities of food (jacket potatoes, black sausage, gherkins, bread and two whole roast chickens) plus a barful of vodka and beer.

"We're all in one house here," cried Zhore expansively, "so help yourselves." An hour later, Zhore bought a bottle of champagne from a passing salesman. By 8.30 (the train had left at 7.00pm) Paul's voice was thick and slurry and his eyes misty; he leaned back and beamed like a Cheshire cat. As the compartment got steamier, we peeled off layers of clothing. (Was this becoming a habit?) Vika dove under a sheet and emerged in a skimpy pink nightdress, from which her ample flesh bulged invitingly. She was the first one to settle into her bunk and promptly fell asleep on her back. We three talked quietly on the opposite seat. I suddenly sensed that Paul's attention was elsewhere, and realised that he was staring fixedly at the seat opposite. Vika had kicked off her sheet, her nightdress had climbed up her hips, and all was revealed. Zhore appeared not to notice! We all keeled over after midnight. I was rudely awakened at 7.30 am by a smart slap on my bottom and a bellowed "Hi-Yi-Zayter!" It transpired that this day was the Russian New Year, as they first celebrate the new calendar and then the old one.

Zhore insisted on my downing a glass of vodka before I'd even opened my eyes, which nearly killed me

I woke from a mid-morning snooze to find Zhore and Vika gone. In their place were a rather nice man who worked for the Red Cross and his 14-year-old son. They had been travelling all the way from Irkutsk in Siberia and were on their way to Rostov to celebrate the New Year with the man's parents.

The journey for the two of them cost seven million roubles! (It took me a while to get used to the fact that one of the first things a Russian would ask was how much you earned and other questions related to money, and how open they were about this topic.)

A little later, an attractive, well-dressed Russian in his late twenties joined us from another compartment. He spoke excellent English and had worked three years for an

American company that supplied pipes for gas and fuel. He said that in the previous eight months the Russians had completely stopped spending money on infrastructure and as a result his branch would shortly be closed.

I've always enjoyed travelling in long-distance trains. As well as getting to know one's travelling companions in a short space of time– indeed, in some countries one creates a sort of 'family' for the duration of the journey, the 'ties' generally being broken the instant one's feet touch the platform of destination – you can learn much about a country by peering out of the window. The lines pass straight by farms and homes whose occupants carry on, apparently oblivious of the curious eyes of passengers.

The snow was also thick in Rostov. The electric train took well over two hours to reach Taganrog and was absolutely freezing. It soon became clear that no trams were running so we trudged through the snow. By the time we reached Rosa Luxemburg Street my hands and feet were in the first stages of frostbite. As they began to thaw, I ran about the kitchen like a demented chicken, shrieking with pain.

9 Goodbye Rosa Luxemburg

It was good to get back to work. I read my more advanced students a poem entitled 'Hard Frost' by Andrew Young, as it seemed rather appropriate. Russians know their own poetry well and generally love reciting; their language is very soft and fluid and lends itself well to this medium. During the Stalinist era, poetry was an important form of communication because it was not considered politically dangerous. This is rather ironic when you trouble to read poets like Mayakovsky.

One day I called on Valya as she was unwell, bringing some fruit and aromatherapy oils with me. We were quietly talking in the living room when her husband, Genio, suddenly shot into the room bellowing "Fuck off!" several times. I was taken aback as I didn't think he ever swore, even in Russian. Actually, he was shouting something rather innocuous in

Russian because he had inadvertently flooded the kitchen.

Some Russian sounds are difficult for us, as they use the front of the mouth and lips much more than we do, and also delicately curl the tongue tip up to the central palate to make soft curling sounds. Many Russian speakers have full, very elastic lips because they use their lips so much in speech, whereas an English speaker can speak and barely move the lips at all (witness the Royal family). Apparently, British sailors who did the Atlantic run to Russian ports during the last war were advised to greet Russians with the words: "Does yer arse fit?" spoken fast, which sounded sufficiently like the Russian "hello" (zdrazdvootye).

I was lucky with my first winter in Russia. It was colder than anywhere I'd ever been, but the sky was generally a clear blue and it was almost always sunny. The snow was deliciously crunchy as I regularly walked to the sea. There were kids with toboggans and younger siblings swaddled like stuffed teddy bears with their little arms sticking straight out because they couldn't bend them. The sea was frozen to the horizon and walking on it was like treading on brittle biscuits.

Outside our yard gate, someone had stuck an enormous 'slate' of ice, about the size and shape of a curve-topped tombstone. The snow must have drifted against a brick wall originally as it still retained the marks of the bricks.

I let myself into the house and found Vitaly in the kitchen. He was not looking happy and I asked him what was wrong. "Chorni i byeli" (black and white) he replied. He then added drily that Olga was an icecream (marozhonoe) – maroz meaning 'frost' and zhena 'wife'. Vitaly then asked what we called an ice on a stick. "A lolly", I replied. He then told me he had a 'frost wife on sticklike legs'. He loved wordplay, as did many of the Russians I met.

Paul and I had been living in the attic flat for two months, and it became ever clearer that Olga had a mental condition – probably manic depression. In her negative moods she treated Vitaly like a slave, forbidding him from using any furniture because it was hers and not his. She also lurked in the flat while we were trying to prepare lessons, ineffectively wiping the floorboards with a disgusting rag.

On one such occasion, Paul barked at her that she was interfering with his work, and she offered to clean for a fee. Paul readily complied but stupidly didn't agree on a figure. A week later she demanded a ridiculous amount for her 'work', which consisted of running her rag over the floor once a week.

We consulted Valya on the going rate and she threw up her hands in horror, crying that the figure was 'absolutely outrageous'.

When we challenged Olga she got very difficult. Valya and Anya came round to reason with her. I wish I had had recording equipment to hand. The three women were at it for hours hammer and tongs. They were all shouting simultaneously, throwing their arms about, rolling their eyeballs and rolling their r's. They were gloriously theatrical.

After reviling one another without mercy, they finally embraced, addressed one another with pet names, and went their ways looking immensely pleased.

Shortly after this, Anya informed us that she had found a replacement flat and we would be moving soon. I found the state of affairs both sad and comic as I loved Vitaly and was fond of Olga in her saner moments, but Paul had no time for her and was keen to move.

The very next morning, I was surprised to find a stranger sitting at the kitchen table eating breakfast. I realised he was a B&B

customer: Olga certainly didn't waste any time when it came to money!

I was so astonished by the size of his breakfast that I made a point of passing the table a couple of times so that I could make a mental list of the food he was consuming.

He had two large cups of lemon tea, a bottle of beer, five good-sized slices of smoked ham, five large boiled potatoes, three large gherkins, seven sausages (four large frankfurters and three short, fat ones), eight thick slices of white bread and about six cloves of raw garlic. He cleared all but three slices of bread. I knew that Russians considered breakfast an important meal but …….! We moved out a week later.

10 Our First Move

It was early February, and the snow had been trampled into ice that was treacherous. I noticed that many old women had strapped wooden soles with nails to their boots, which seemed wise. A few days before we moved, Paul slipped on the ice and broke his right hand. What timing!

As a result of Paul's accident, the first few weeks were exhausting. In addition to teaching, I had to do all the shopping, cooking, cleaning and laundry, do up Paul's shoelaces and buttons daily, and take a considerably longer journey to work as the new flat was on the Taganrog outskirts. I also had to spend several hours over several days at the dentist having a tooth reconstructed. On the bright side, the flat was spacious and furnished and it was all our own. The loo and basin leaked, but not much, and the twin-tub washing machine (what luxury) turned out to be a white elephant.

When I attempted to use it, it gave off a terrible burning smell, which hung around for hours, wouldn't spin, and refused to drain itself. I spent over an hour emptying it with a small plastic scoop!

My bedroom was furnished with huge chests of drawers and cupboards but they were stuffed to bursting with the owners' possessions, so I continued to live out of my suitcase. This troubled me not at all. Having run a home in England for many years, it was a relief to have the minimum of housework, few possessions, and practically no modern 'conveniences'. It made me realise how we twenty-first century haves weigh ourselves down with what we are persuaded will make our lives easier.

The laundry was done once a week in the bath. I threw everything into hot, sudsy water, stamped on the soggy mass with bare feet, left it to soak, rinsed it all and hung it out. No ironing.

The floor was swept with a twig broom, and the rugs (there were no fitted carpets, thank goodness) were occasionally heaved outside and hung over the communal metal 'lines' to be beaten with whatever long whacking tool one could find. For best effect, one laid them on the ground, covered them with snow and left them for several hours before beating the snow off. Eureka! Bright good-as-new rugs.

I was keen to observe how the locals organised things. How, for instance, did they deal with icy draughts?

The solution was simple and, again, very cheap. You made a paste with flour and water and then pressed the dough round the edges of all the windows.

This actually formed an excellent seal. And it didn't mean that you couldn't get any fresh air, either, as some of the windows had a very small window set into the glass which could be opened separately. Ingenious.

One Friday, Paul and I were shuffling along the icy pavement towards the tram stop. At one point, the pavement rose steeply before levelling out again, and each time Paul attempted to reach the top he slid back. I tried to push him from behind and we both nearly came to grief. Friday was the day my precious weekly Guardian was delivered to the school, and I had it in my bag. I had a silent tussle with myself. I knew that if I spread the newspaper on the ice it would make the climb much easier and safer for Paul. I also knew that the paper would almost certainly stick to the ice and be ruined! I'm glad to say that my honourable side won the day. Rather like the famous story of Sir Walter Raleigh laying his valuable cloak over a puddle for Good Queen Bess, I laid my newspaper on the pavement and enabled Paul to continue his walk unscathed.

I did manage to scrape a few dog-eared pages off the pavement but the crossword, alas, was beyond saving.

Towards the end of March, when Paul was out of plaster, we decided to throw a party for some of our Russian friends. We baked two huge meat loaves, and a nut roast, made devilled eggs and devils on horseback (soaked prunes wrapped in bacon), mixed a variety of salads and spread yellow caviar on black bread. There were about twenty guests. The girls were all rather modest and sat in a row on one of the beds, but the men got very merry. Grigori taught me a vigorous Cossack dance; Igor sang some melancholy traditional songs to the accompaniment of his guitar, and Dima read our palms. As the men got randier, Volodya made it his business to protect the girls from their advances. It was a grand party and brightened the dark winter month.

11 THE CAUCASUS

I had two holidays coming up: a week at the end of March and the national May holiday. I decided to visit my penfriend Marina, if it suited her, in May and received a positive response from her. But where to go for the March holiday? I consulted my Lonely Planet Guide and thought that Kislovodsk or Pyatigorsk in the Caucasus sounded like nice places. I consulted my students who were generally discouraging: "It is dangerous. There are avalanches now. There are terrorists. You might be shot or taken hostage." They really were incredibly alarmist, but I decided to go anyway, and plumped for Kislovodsk. Of course, many of the countries that were part of the Soviet Union in the south had been fighting for independence– Chechnya in particular – so it was perhaps understandable that Russians should view these areas with suspicion. I tried to convince my more liberal-minded students that most mountain races are not savages, but proud, independent people who survive in a particularly tough and inhospitable environment. If you meet them on their own ground and treat them with respect, they can prove extraordinarily hospitable.

I took a night train to the Caucasus. It was very hot in the compartment and I slept not a wink. I shared my food with a nice man who, in his turn, offered me delicious apricot pastries, green bottled tomatoes and spiced fish courtesy of his wife.

At Kislovodsk station I enquired the way to the hotel mentioned in my guide that wasn't overly expensive, and caught a bus there. I had a moment's mild panic when I checked in. The large, rather fearsome looking receptionist asked to see my visa, which I hadn't got. With slightly quailing heart, I bluffed innocence and said I didn't need one as I was only staying three days before I returned to work in Taganrog. This worked, fortunately.

My room was comfortable, with a good bed, a huge fridge and TV, a desk and armchair and a wardrobe with HANGERS! However, the shower patently hadn't worked for ages: the shower head was rusty and the floor outlet blocked.

After unpacking, I took a walk round Kislovodsk, which is a spa town. It is extremely elegant with a lot of handsome wooden buildings with enormous balconies, and some rather gothic-looking buildings in the centre. The town is in a high valley surrounded by rather strange-shaped hills, which are clearly volcanic. Some of them look a bit like slag heaps that are flattened on top. Groups of old men were gathered on public benches, many playing backgammon at incredible speed. There were a lot of blue firs, which looked most ethereal. I noticed that the blue tits and coal tits had slightly different head markings from the British varieties.

I visited the Narzan Springs, housed in a handsome marble hall. There were about fifteen different varieties of spa water. I tasted the water from one tap after another. Some of them were extremely sulphurous and rather disgusting, while others were delicious. I bought some plastic bottles from an old woman and filled them with the waters I liked.

I then took a leisurely walk through an enormous park. Everything was bright and crisp under a fresh fall of snow, and there were many red squirrels. I rode a cable car to the top of Mount Meloe Sedlo though, sadly, a heavy mist reduced visibility considerably.

On my return to the hotel, I asked the receptionist if my shower could be mended.

To my surprise, a pleasant man knocked on my door ten minutes later and put the shower to rights.

After two hours' work on my Russian (nobody seemed to speak English here) I decided to 'hit town'. I dolled myself up – earrings, make-up, perfume, the lot – and strolled down to the centre. It was snowing heavily and looked pretty by moonlight. There were few people around, most of them militia, probably doing their military service. They seemed friendly and very young.

The first restaurant I tried was empty, the second was just closing (at 6.30 pm!), so I finally selected a rather smart restaurant opposite Narzan Springs. I spent a good while trying to make sense of the menu with the aid of my huge dictionary and chose well. I started with a tasty fungi salad with herbs, raw onion and a dressing, followed by a heavenly borsch which was a meal in itself. All washed down with an iced martini, and two cups of excellent coffee with cognac. The next morning I took a taxi to the Alikanovki Gorge and asked the pleasant driver to pick me up in front of the Zamok Restaurant at 4.00.

The gorge was a wild, deserted place with sheer yellow rock walls and a fast-flowing river. I walked several miles without seeing another soul, and returned to the restaurant with an immense appetite.

It was in a splendid sort of castle named The Castle of Treachery and Love, so-called because a shepherd boy is said to have fallen in love with a rich girl and they were, of course, forbidden to marry. They made a death pact to leap from the top of the gorge. He jumped first; she saw the mess, and didn't. The taxi driver arrived on time, and I found a big Communist rally in full swing on my return. On Saturday, I caught the 8.42 am train to Taganrog. It was a bright sunny day with a real feeling of spring. Once clear of the rather uncompromising Caucasus foothills, I saw people digging and sowing everywhere. There was a brilliant green in some of the fields – my first Russian green – amid rich black earth, still striped with snow by the hedges and windbreaks. Chickens were scraping and grooming themselves in dirt bowls, and there were many geese and Muscovy ducks. We passed several gigantic metal towers – silos, I guessed.

There were many stops, the best of which was Kavkazkaya, clearly an important rail junction. The platform was teeming with people selling local produce and I bought a delicious cold fried fish for 300 roubles. There were several enormous train sheds, loads of engines, carriages and cargo trucks and great yellow cranes. And the biggest railway turntable I had ever seen: it had about ten huge engines on it.

Back in Taganrog, I took a long walk through the town and alongside the sea. A herd of goats were leaping and cavorting in mock fights. Bright yellow aconites and shy violets were flowering everywhere, and leaf buds were swollen to bursting point. The town would soon exult in a wash of delicate green tracery everywhere.

To celebrate, I bought a large bag of dried chamomile from a Ukrainian woman and soaked some of it in a basin of warm water until it was golden green. I first washed my tired eyes with it, then washed my hair in it, and finally poured the residue into the bath and soaked in it. Lovely! The water in town was terrible and my hair had suffered as a result: dry, stringy and lank.

12 The Republic of Georgia

Although I'd just had a short break, I needed to organise my main holiday in Georgia. My penfriend Marina had told me that she could obtain a Georgian visa for me from a friend who worked in the Tbilisi embassy, but friends in Taganrog warned me that I would still need an entry\exit visa, which I could only obtain in Rostov. Anya kindly offered to accompany me to Rostov. The two of us took an early bus to the city on Tuesday and then waited for ages in a dingy hall. The visa people weren't very helpful and said I'd have to leave my passport with them and return the next day. I replied that that was impossible because of work so we agreed on Thursday at 11.00 am.

I trailed back to Rostov – this time with Olya Bondarenko, Anya's charming and gentle part-time assistant. At first we were the only people waiting, then the room began to fill up – and how!

The office didn't open till almost midday, but we were seen first.

The office was manned by a military gentleman sporting a great many medals on his generous chest. He couldn't understand why I wanted to go to Tbilisi and kept trying to persuade me to go to Lake Baikal. The upshot was that I got absolutely nowhere and clearly was not going to receive an entry/exit visa. I left in a rage, taking my passport with me.

On my return, I asked Anya if she could give me an official letter saying I worked for the school and must return by x date, and she agreed. A few days later the dear lady handed me a splendidly official-looking document, stating that I was indispensable to the school, and bearing an impressive stamp.

The following morning I went to the Aeroflot office in Taganrog with Paul's lovely girlfriend, Lena, who insisted on coming with me. Having been fiercely independent most of my life, I was learning to gratefully accept help offered from Russian friends and colleagues. In a country with such a heavy-handed bureaucracy, it was reassuring - and calming– to have the support of someone who knew the ropes, or at least spoke the language more proficiently than me.

I couldn't believe it! The officials in the Aeroflot Office wouldn't sell me an air ticket. Why not? Because they didn't know what to charge me for it!! As a foreigner, I had to pay more – but how much more? I would have to go to Rostov Airport to buy my ticket. Oh, how I was beginning to hate Rostov

Three days later I was once again on a bus to Rostov, but solo this time. The airport was a dreary building absolutely crawling with militia. I eventually found the ticket office and explained the situation. The ticket lady didn't know what to charge me either, though she made several phone calls to try and find out. She then informed me that I would have to return another day, as the boss was unavailable. At this point I lost my rag. A rather nice American businessman, who had been trying to purchase a ticket to Tbilisi for three days to sell mobile telephones, tugged my arm and begged me to calm down.

He was probably afraid my rage would kybosh his own faint chance of success.

However, my theatricals did appear to get me somewhere. The woman disappeared for a while and, on her return, said they would organise a ticket for me and send it to the

Aeroflot office in Taganrog for collection. I could pay there.

Four days later, the local Aeroflot office phoned me to confirm that my return ticket had arrived. Two weeks later, on 6th May, I was on the electric train to Rostov. As my plane was due to depart at 8.00 am, I planned to spend a boring night in the airport, but this was not to be. An armed military policeman barred my way and told me the airport was closed until 6 am and I would have to spend the night in the Airport Hotel across the car park. It was a most inhospitable building, overseen by a dragon of a woman who actually wasn't as fierce as she looked. My room was bare, cold, none too clean, and waterless. I couldn't sleep, so I trundled out into the long corridor. A man in his mid-thirties was sitting smoking on a very tatty armchair at one end of the corridor, so I joined him. He was a pilot and very chatty. I eventually got a bit of shut-eye and walked over to the airport at 6.30, though I needn't have bothered. There was nowhere to get so much as a cup of coffee and there was no mention of the flight to Tbilisi until 9.00, an hour later than the scheduled departure. I amused myself by watching a solemn little man laying out an odd assortment of items for sale on a small folding table. He spent a good half hour moving them around, standing back to survey his handiwork, and then making minor adjustments.

Nobody bought anything, nor even stopped to glance at his wares.

I found his particularity and perseverance admirable, and rather sad.

When at last the plane was ready for boarding, there were no checks of any kind and we passengers hefted our luggage onto a small plane c/o Don Avia Airline. Half the seats didn't appear to be fixed to anything and rocked violently as the plane took off. The tail section was laid out like a small lounge, with a couple of sofas and what looked suspiciously like a mini-bar, and was full of military personnel. We civilians were all herded into the front end. The stewardess took no notice of any of us and spent the entire flight flirting and drinking with the soldiers.

I wouldn't have been surprised to discover that the pilot was also carousing in the tail, leaving our wispy craft to its own devices! The plane was supposed to make a half-hour stop at a place called Elista, which according to my guide was north-east of the Caucasus Mountains. I was therefore puzzled when we flew over a snow-covered range of mountains without landing in Elista first.

Then I saw a large city below us, glowing in sunshine in a beautiful valley surrounded by mountains. We landed, and everyone disembarked. It was only then that I realised we had reached Tbilisi. What happened to Elista?

My visa was waiting for me and cost US $70. I also changed 150,000 roubles for 50 laris. As there was no sign of Marina, I decided to take a taxi to her address, which cost 40 laris. I had a nasty feeling I had not brought sufficient money with me. The lar was apparently almost worthless.

I was given a warm welcome by Marina, her mother, and her younger sister Kate. Marina looked typically Georgian – dark-eyed, with black hair and a prominent Semitic nose.

She was small and slender and seemed gentle and reserved.

I had taken advice from friends in Taganrog as to the best gifts to bring, and had brought a bag full of goodies as well as several books in English for Marina.

Marina was delighted with the books, but I got the impression that bringing food was not in order.

We sat down to a huge meal of dolmades (pancakes stuffed with cream cheese and minced beef) and a delicious home-made chocolate and hazelnut cake. It was soon clear that I was not going to be allowed to do anything – not so much as wash a teacup. Marina insisted that I sleep in her room, while she slept on the sofa bed in the sitting room. Both she and her mother had taken a week off work on my behalf, which I'm sure they could ill afford.

I knew that Georgia has a very ancient and interesting history. The Christian Church was established very early there, and one of the oldest vines for wine was discovered there. Georgians drink amazing quantities of wine and have a reputation for long life. The Georgian alphabet is extraordinary – I've never seen another like it - and apparently bears a number of resemblances to the oldest known written language.

The language is soft and front-of-throatish with quite a lot of guttural sounds, rather like Arabic.

I also knew that Stalin was Georgian, and his mother was Christian. Beyond that, I didn't know much.

The next morning Marina drove me on a tour in her 20-year-old Lada, affectionately named Za-Za.

Tbilisi is a beautiful city in a stunning location. It winds along three or four valleys with steep-sided cliffs and hills on every side, and the brown River Kura snaking through it. She drove north out of the city, following the course of the River Mtkvari through a wide and lush valley, which gradually became narrower and steeper. Lots of woolly sheep and goats were being herded up the valley to summer pastures, and little wooden houses clung to the hillsides. In the villages, delightful hairy pigs and piglets rooted round and held up any traffic.

Many fruit trees were in blossom. It all looked wonderfully fertile and picturesque.

Our first stop was a beautiful fourth century church on the edge of a high cliff, looking over the Mtkvari River to the town of Mtsketa, which was the capital of Georgia until the fifth century. The high pastures were a glory of wild poppies, pungent herbs and shrubs and the whistling of many varieties of birds. The air was clean and clear.

We stopped for a picnic lunch at the monastery church of Ananuri: a fine complex of brick and stone buildings enclosed within a fortified wall. The wall paintings had long gone, but there were some excellent stone carvings, the motifs of which put me in mind of Celtic scrollwork. After a leisurely lunch and stroll, we drove on up to the narrow end of the valley to a place called Pasanauri, where we had a magnificent view of the snow-capped peaks of the main Caucasus range. We followed the course of the Avagri River which, at one point, rather dramatically joins another river. The water of one is clear and 'white', while the other is dark and 'black', so that at their confluence the water is delightfully striped.

We made a final stop at Mtsketa, where we visited two more ancient churches, one of which had a little chapel dedicated to Santa Nino who first brought Christianity to Georgia and converted the then king and queen.

The next day, after visiting the Institute of Foreign Affairs, where Marina worked, and talking to her students, we took a long walk around the city. We rode the funicular railway to the top of a hill, from which there was a stunning view of the whole city.

The once handsome building at the top was empty and in ruins, and the public gardens were neglected. Marina became quite agitated and two great tears plopped down her cheeks.

She admitted that it was the first time she had been there since the civil war began 5-6 years before and she couldn't bear to see one of her favourite places in such a dismal state. Apparently the ruined building used to be a fine restaurant and tea room. I pointed out that there was still plenty to admire about the site and, when the loudspeakers suddenly produced some frightful 'music' – the system was clearly faulty and was mostly whines and fuzz- I grinned and suggested that they were doing their best to please us both. She laughed ruefully.

It was beginning to dawn on me that this beautiful country was suffering difficult times.

I discovered that, with the collapse of the old Soviet Union, Georgia became an independent republic. This new country claimed Tbilisi's authority over the regions of Ossetia and Abkhazia, which led to four years of vicious civil war.

Russia supported the independence of Ossetia and Abkhazia, which sparked off war with Russia too.

The country was still reeling and its infrastructure was in a parlous state. There were regular electricity cuts, shortages of water, and many of the roads were in a dreadful condition, yet the people were making the best of a bad job, Marina's family in particular.

Another thing that interested me was that Georgia had been under Persian and Turkish domination for long periods, and is still surrounded by Muslim countries, and yet it has remained strongly Christian. There are Orthodox churches everywhere, and they are well attended.

On Friday Marina drove us to her dacha in the hills, near a village called Panamori (wild pear). The road surface was terrible and on some of the hairpin bends nearly half the road had slid down the cliffs, but Marina handled Za-Za with loving care and we reached her dacha in one piece. It was a dear little cabin on the side of a hill, overlooking woods and snow-capped mountains. I saw rollers and redstarts and a host of wild flowers. Marina visibly softened and relaxed. She clearly loved this place.

As we sat on the ground eating barbecued meat, I asked her whether it would be possible to hear some Georgian 3-part singing, as they are famed for this.

She replied that, regrettably, there were no concerts at this time of year. That night, back in Tbilisi, the Lord answered my prayer. I was awoken at about 2.00 a.m. by the sound of male voices raised in song.

At first I thought that a neighbour must be playing the radio very loud, but then something told me this was local and spontaneous. I crept onto the balcony. A group of about eight men in the courtyard below, seated around a table with their wine, were singing their traditional songs in three parts.

It was an absolute joy to hear them. I'm ashamed to say that I had to lie to Marina. Her mother, Lina's, cooking was amazing, but she always insisted on giving me a second helping, and I was beginning to feel that I would burst open like a fried sausage.

So I asked Marina to tell Lina that I had a recurrent stomach complaint and that the best remedy was to starve myself for a day or two. I didn't want to offend anyone, and luckily this worked.

Marina told me that she was going to take me to visit her cousins in a village called Signaxi to the east of Tbilisi, and we took a bus there.

Signaxi (the 'x' pronounced like 'ch' as in 'loch') is a spectacular village perched high on a spur that juts out into the flat riverain plain of the Alazani River. As everywhere in this country, the Caucasus Mountains rose up sheer, snow-covered and ethereal.

Marina's relatives had a big, airy house with a large and well-stocked garden, and were most hospitable. The man of the house was a psychologist, an interesting and erudite gentleman, and there were three adult sons.

Marina was evidently very fond of them all and became much more relaxed and playful. One of the sons – Georgi – wanted to show me a video, but there wasn't enough power. He tinkered with some solar panels and a battery and eventually succeeded in raising sufficient wattage.

The water pressure was zero, too, so Georgi had erected a sort of electric foot pedal pump to produce a trickle of water. This had been the way of things for the past three years apparently.

We took the bus back to Tbilisi on Sunday morning, arriving in time to attend a service in Marina's local church.

It was a lovely old church, choc-a-bloc with frescoes, triptychs, paintings, and gold, and the singing was good. A red-robed priest wandered round, wildly swinging an incense burner.

As there were a lot of gold doors and screens, he kept disappearing and then popping out somewhere else: it was a bit like a seventeenth century farce! As the service was long – over two hours – I wandered outside at one point. It is perfectly acceptable to do this in the Greek Orthodox Church.

There were several women begging. A young boy with an angelic smile and empty eyes was slowly and concentratedly pushing a cardboard box around the square. On a balcony, a very old man, gaunt and with paper-white skin, was slowly and gracefully dancing all by himself to inaudible music. In the evening, I asked Marina if she would sing some Georgian songs for me.

I knew she played the guitar. At first she shyly refused, but her mother added her pleas to mine. First she sang some simple English nursery rhymes to a guitar accompaniment, and I sang along with her.

She had a sweet clear voice. She soon forgot her shyness and she and Lina sang several Georgian songs. I soon picked up the tunes and joined in with the missing third part. The music brought us all very close. It was delightful. We ended our celebration with clove tea, white cherries and quinces in syrup, sweet pickled walnuts and bread and cheese. They both accompanied me to the airport on Monday morning and we had emotional farewells. I enormously liked them both, and their country, and prayed that it would soon be restored to its former glory, after years of trials.

On arrival in Taganrog airport, I had half an hour of anxiety when an official scanned the formal letter from Anya, frowned, told me to wait to one side, and disappeared. Would it work or not? It did work, thankfully. And a huge thank you to Anya.

I had four further weeks of teaching, in intense heat, until the term ended at the end of June. I had agreed to return for the next teaching year, beginning in September, and Paul was also returning. Anya told us that the flat would be available for us, so we could leave possessions there, which was a great relief.

My first seven months had been a solid learning experience. I had worked very hard at becoming an effective EFL teacher with my own particular style, had gradually familiarised myself with the geography of the town and its facilities; worked on the Russian language and culture, and built some sound working relationships. I had also made a small handful of true friends. I had begun to feel a real connection with this shabby yet oddly magnetic town and I hoped that in my second year I could develop deeper personal relationships and take a more active part in the life of the town.

As I travelled back to Moscow – for once a remarkably quiet journey – I had leisure to mull on the fact that I felt so happy in south-west Russia despite the drawbacks. I realised that I had felt able to truly discover myself– my inner self. Nobody there knew anything about my past, nor did they have prior expectations. They welcomed me, offered me their help and friendship and accepted me just as I was in the Now.

The work was fulfilling and my lifestyle was simple. I felt I had space to grow. And grow, I decided, I would, God willing.

13 WE MOVE AGAIN

Paul and I returned to Taganrog mid-September 1997. It was good to be back.

Two weeks into the term, my student Volodya invited me to Sunday lunch with his family, suggesting we meet outside the school gate at midday. I duly arrived, dressed in a smart, tightish skirt, a flimsy top and lightweight slip-ons, with handbag, chocolates and flowers. It was bright and windy. To my surprise, instead of walking to their flat, we walked down to the port, where a small group of people (some known to me, most not) were waiting. It transpired that they had booked a yacht for the day from the Yacht Club. We boarded the boat via an extremely decrepit and unsteady floating jetty, with plenty of missing slats and wide gaps between each floating platform. I'm a Capricorn goat and am not usually concerned about such things, but I was unsuitably dressed for leaping over deep water. I was greatly relieved to gain the relatively stable deck without embarrassment.

Including crew, there were about twelve of us. There was a brisk breeze as we set sail and I soon got terribly cold. However, one kind soul found me a snug old sweater and a blanket, after which I thoroughly enjoyed the trip. Everyone brought bags stuffed with food and drink, there was much talk and laughter and, in the early evening, we started to sing, recite poetry and recount tales.

A few days later, in early October, Anya moved us to a new flat in the centre of town with practically no warning. I knew by this time that it was not uncommon for Russian families to let their homes for a period if times were hard. They would move in with other family members, taking only those items they really needed. This would explain why our previous flat had so much unnecessary furniture, absolutely stuffed with possessions not our own.

The flat was in a good location nearer the town centre and the main beach but was otherwise barely liveable.

Apparently, the landlady – a horrendous woman with a strident voice, dyed red hair and a very meek husband - had promised to finish decorating and install a phone and other necessities before we moved in, but…..when we first arrived, just after wobbling upright after a brief bout of 'flu, we had no bedding, a non-working fridge, and a water heater that very nearly blew us sky-high, after which it was pots of water on the stove and cold showers.

The sink and basin both leaked, most of the lights didn't work and the flat was only half papered – though, frankly, who cared about décor and gracious living? All we needed was a bit of light and warmth.

Our contract specified a fully furnished flat but what did that mean in Russia? My bedroom boasted a child-size sort of camp bed (luckily, I am child-sized) and a desk with no accompanying chair or lamp. As usual, nowhere to store anything. In Paul's room there was a large wardrobe, a very dicey double divan which didn't look as if it would bear his weight for long, a bookcase unit and two chairs.

Most of our energies, after and before work, were spent in trying to sort things out. Our landlady was undoubtedly a crook but it seemed we would eventually win out.

She would turn up at unexpected moments (usually with obedient husband in tow), bearing gifts. To wit: two enormous pans with lids; one middle-sized non-stick pan containing about an inch of sloppy oil and a lid full of cobwebs; one enamel bowl too large to fit into either sink or basin; one eiderdown which was so thin one wondered what exactly happened to the eider?

We went down to the market our first weekend and bought useful kitchen utensils.

Over the next few weeks, the landlady arrived unannounced, often with one or two burly men, bringing odd bits of furniture and, eventually, the kalonka (water heater), the leaks and the light fittings were put to rights. Her visits gradually decreased, and then, thankfully, ceased altogether.

The weather was getting noticeably colder, so Paul and I spent the best part of one Saturday taping cracks in the window panes, and cramming strips of newspaper dipped in a flour paste into all the gaps and crannies round the window frames. The flat was then surprisingly warm and comfortable.

It was also only a ten-minute walk from the main beach, which meant that I could take regular dips and runs in the early morning, which was invigorating.

Our other main concern at that time was to support a new teacher, Jonathan, who was in his mid-twenties and rather shy. He had been studying Russian in England for some time and had spent a month in Moscow with his brother. On his first day at school, he was pounced on by one of the Russian teachers at the day school, who clung to him like a limpet, hovering in the hall and waiting to snap him up as soon as our lessons ended. He was living with a Russian family in another part of town.

In early December, he came round to our flat in a bit of a state and admitted that he didn't know what to do about the amorous advances of the teacher. We gave him plenty of moral support and told him he would need to be 'cruel to be kind'.

I had made friends with a Russian English teacher, Sonya, who invited me to lunch in her flat. It was a nice flat with lovely furniture – all made by her husband, Ivan.

He used to be an ace fighter pilot, and showed me interesting photos, in one of which he was wearing a suit like an astronaut's. He did actually meet some of them. Though he was an excellent pilot, he was never allowed to fly outside Russian territory. Why? Because he was married to Sonya. Most of the men on her father's side were excellent linguists, several of whom were 'purged' by Stalin and simply disappeared. Ivan had been made redundant two years previously, just before his entitlement to a considerable pension. He couldn't find another suitable job and so retired at 42, and spent most of his time making furniture and hunting with his spaniel. Their freezer was stacked to the gunnels with deer and other carcasses.

I took a walk at the weekend to the old Taganrog fishing village, which was the original town. There was a tiny church, which had recently been renovated.

What local artists perhaps lacked in talent they certainly made up for in jollity. There were frescoes of lots of multi-winged angels that looked rather like 1920s debutantes in pink and blue feather boas!

Outside the church I saw quite possibly the oldest woman in Taganrog. She was completely toothless, about three feet nothing and very thin, with a beaky nose and chin that almost met in the middle, like fairy tale pictures of witches. Her pale skin was like fine wrinkled parchment, but her small, bright black eyes were like a robin's and it was clear that she was known and much-loved by the local people.

In this old village there were no neat grids but a maze of narrow alleys and footpaths, with a jumble of little one-storey cottages brightly painted white, dark green, bright blue and terracotta. They had heavy wooden shutters, brick fluting surrounded by neat vine trellises, and higgledy-piggledy sheds. The port was full of boats, and there were groups everywhere of old men and women on benches, chattering like starlings.

14 Ice on Land and Sea

On the 15th of December the temperature dropped to -10^{0}C. The pavements were like crystal – smooth, glassy and gleaming – and extremely treacherous. Trees were splitting and cracking. There were frequent electricity cuts, due to cables being sliced by sharp ice crystals. The wind was sharp and dry and, when it gusted, one skimmed helplessly along like a sand yacht out of control. Many old women strapped spiked plates under the soles of their boots. I heard that one poor man slipped whilst jumping off a tram and got both his legs sliced off by the tram wheels.

The very next day the temperature plummeted to -20^{0}C. The sky was bright blue round a wintry sun; the air so cold and dry that it burned your skin. It felt great at first – so stimulating. Then the wind snarled you and flayed your cheeks; your eyes watered and the water instantly froze. Your body temperature took a dive so you couldn't feel feet or hands.

All flexibility gone, you slid helplessly along the pavement, flatfooted and slow. The brain literally seemed to curdle. "Can't think. Slow. Slide. Slither. Slow." You reached home and fumbled with the door key – no strength in frozen fingers to turn the lock. When at last you succeeded, you peeled off gloves and clumsily unzipped boots.

Sensation began to flow like a seeping scald. "Ouch! Ouch!" Fingers were purple. You whimpered like a whipped puppy. Head and eyelids heavy. "Oh, boil kettle, boil! I want that steaming cup of tea!" Outside the window, a fallen tree groaned and creaked like a creature in pain.

One of the electricity cuts occurred on a Saturday evening when our friends Ina and Vova, a married couple who were students of Paul's, were visiting. We had failed to buy candles or a torch (soon to be corrected!). Quite unfazed, one of them lit matches one by one, whilst the other deftly scooped a hole in a couple of raw potatoes, made wicks by twisting a strip of lint I had in the bathroom, poured in some cooking oil and – bingo! – we had efficient candles. I do love the intrepid way Russians deal with any inconvenience.

I guess generations of shortages and hardship have made them inventive.

A few days later I took a walk down the old stairs to the beach. It was a bright, crisp day.

There was a wide channel of water like a dark scar in the sea ice – still and mirror-reflective, and the ice was grey and opaque.

The port cranes and factory chimneys were softly reflected in the water, for the harbour was always kept clear of ice– not just for the ships, but also for the hardy Russians who chose to swim daily throughout the winter. It was truly a world of the five elements: the ice, water and clear air; fire represented by the poplars with their 'charred' black trunks and bare branches and by the drooping willows with their flaming red branches.

The Azov Sea is a strange sea. At its greatest depth it reaches 20 m and, because the great River Don flows into the sea a little east of Taganrog, the water along the east coast is not salty.

In summer, a vigorous weed turns the water a soupy pea-green and, if you dare to dunk yourself, you will emerge resembling an elf from A Midsummer Night's Dream. In winter it regularly freezes and becomes a winter playground.

Families take a stroll on the ice; groups of teenagers clear patches for ice hockey; there are skaters and, of course, there are the ice fishermen.

Fishing is a popular pastime for men throughout the year and 'a little ice' doesn't deter them.

On winter weekends you can see them strung out against the skyline, providing a focus for ice-blind eyes.

Their tools are few, and homemade more often than not: a small sledge, an eccentric 'snow bike' or a little folding stool to perch on; a hand drill to bore holes in the ice; a foot-long rod with line and hook, and a little pot of bait; perhaps a bottle of vodka to stave off the cold, and a canvas bag.

The fish they catch are small and look very unappetising: greyly transparent with pale yellow spots on their flanks, blunt noses and fan-shaped dorsal fins. They're thrown onto the ice where they are naturally refrigerated until the fishermen are ready to return home.

The first freeze was succeeded by a partial thaw, with melt pools and a water channel some way offshore. Then, overnight, the temperature plummeted from -4^0C to -26^0C. A new layer of ice about five inches thick, and absolutely transparent, formed over the previous layer.

It was smooth as glass and highly reflective, which created extraordinary optical effects. Hair-thin cracks created by the pressure of moving ice, when struck by the sun, looked like wide strips of bright tin foil and created rainbows, while particles of the earlier ice resembled very fine tissue paper. Through the new surface ice you could clearly see the earlier layer, marked with a tracery of human and dog footprints, sledge and skate trails, icified water snails, sea grass, ferns, reeds and human detritus– all transformed into pure poetry.

As I knelt on the ice, the wind caught my rucksack, slung down beside me, and sent it scudding off like a blue sailboat. Then came a second warm spell. The hairline cracks widened and along these faults great sheets of ice, the size of double doors, were pushed upwards, so that there appeared to be a submerged street of frozen rooftops, homes for Russian ice maidens. The ice moaned and groaned, cricked and cracked.

Every so often there was a drumroll, a fusillade of gunfire, and an 'ice roof' sank majestically into the sea. The ice momentarily vibrated and then there was absolute stillness – until the next collapse.

In places on the ice were round, white patches – slightly domed and delicately patterned with frost flowers. If you trod on one it fragmented instantly with a delicate tinkle. These domes were very fine ice over air pockets.

At the beginning of February there was the first fall of snow and the weather became considerably warmer. I saw an Alsatian quite deliberately and joyfully skating. He whizzed round and round in a tight circle until he got dizzy, then stopped for a moment, rocking from side to side. Then he whizzed round in the opposite direction, 'unwinding' himself. It was comic to watch.

The first of March, officially the first day of spring, was indeed a balmy, sky-blue birdsong day. The remaining sea ice was melting fast; while standing on one floe I found myself gently floating and rocking. There were mini-geysers where trapped air bubbles shot up through cracks in the ice, which broke the surface with a soft shhhh-ing sound. The shiny ice delicately reflected the blue of the sky.

Wherever a decayed leaf, twig or scrap of paper had been embedded, there were enchanting little melt pools, retaining the pattern of whatever the ice had contained.

On 19th March I saw a beautiful wild duck preening itself on one of the remaining ice floes not far offshore. The next day the last of the ice floes had melted, though there was still a strip of crystals along the shore. I noticed something rather odd. When the ice formed, it built up in horizontal layers, but it melted into vertical crystals. If you picked up a handful, it split into ice 'kindling', each strip three to five inches long, and they chinked and tinkled like the facets of a glass chandelier.

By the beginning of April, the temperature had shot up to 38^0C. The numerous apricot, cherry and apple trees had barely had a chance to blossom and – sadly – the spring bulbs, which had shown lush and green, withered in bud in the intense heat. It seemed that 1997 was going to be a year of extremes.

SEA ICE BREAKING UP

15 Christmas and New Year

School broke up on the 24th December. Paul and I had bought a splendid tree and decided to have fun making our own decorations – though we did buy some coloured lights and tinsel. I cut out figures in tin foil, and hangings of coloured tissue paper, but the pièce de résistance was undoubtedly the Christmas fairy on the top. I had treated myself to my first laptop the previous summer in the UK, and Paul enjoyed doing visuals on it. He adapted a picture of a ballerina by adding wings. I then suggested that we had a down-to-earth fairy, so he broadened her. I then set to work with my paints on his print-out. The result was hilarious and much amused our Russian friends. She was a cheerful, rather tarty Madame with bright red frizzy hair and a suspiciously red swollen nose. She was pirouetting unsteadily on one fat leg and wore a tutu and ballet shoes with crossed ribbons. For Christmas dinner, we invited our good friends Ina and Vova, Valya and Genio, and Jonathan for nibbles.

We roasted a large chicken with all the trimmings, as well as devils-on-horseback. I contributed a baked lemon pudding, which was much appreciated, as Russians rarely make puddings and yet adore sweet things. And of course there was plenty of alcohol. It was a lovely evening, crowned for me by a long phone call to my family in the UK. Having rather passed my fiftieth by, I decided to throw a party for my birthday, but without telling my guests that it was in fact my birthday. I invited about twenty people. I decided to make meat loaves, a big dish of liver pâté, and all sorts of salads. Unfortunately, I bought the wrong kind of liver and the pâté was disgusting. In obstinate Capricornian style, instead of ditching it, I kept adding ingredients in hope of improvement, which made it even more revolting! Paul kindly came to my rescue by making curried meatballs, which were delicious. He was a much better cook than I.

As far as I recall, the party was a success and, as usual, vast quantities of alcohol were consumed.

On New Year's Day I called in on my old landlady and landlord, Olga and Vitaly, bearing gifts.

They had obviously just had one of their simmering rows. Vitaly wouldn't open the gate at first, though I could hear him lurking on the other side, so I yelled that it was me. He then let me in, and allowed me to shake his hand, though he didn't say a word and promptly disappeared. However, when I left Olga's 'boudoir' after downing hot raspberry juice and chocolates, I discovered that my muddy boots had been cleaned and polished. Such is distant love, and I was very touched.

Paul and I had been invited to join my student Igor's (of the pink water) family for dinner. They had a lovely old house in the suburbs with a big garden, in which they grew loads of fruit and vegetables. On top of a shed was a very strange structure, which I asked Igor about. It was part of a military aircraft – the tailpiece.

His wife Luda had produced enough food to feed an army, all of it absolutely mouth-watering, and there was some excellent home-brewed wine and liqueurs.

After dinner, Igor played his guitar and sang, we all danced a little and, just before the stroke of midnight, we all went out into the street to see a crazy explosion of bangers, rockets and other fireworks, set off indiscriminately from practically every street, yard and garden the length and breadth of Taganrog. Great fun and no doubt dangerous.

Early in the New Year, Paul told me that he and his girlfriend Lena were engaged.

They decided to hold a party to celebrate and the three of us busied ourselves shopping and cooking for the occasion.

About twenty friends were invited, and Paul gave a touching speech. Lena was looking beautiful and radiant. She was much younger than Paul and they made an odd pair in some ways, but we all wished them happiness. After the party they asked me if I'd mind if Lena moved into our flat. I said that would be fine, though I was secretly a bit anxious about it.

Would we all get on in that small flat?

16 Dogs, Dogs, Dogs

The block of flats we had moved to possessed its own semi-wild dogs. There was a skinny, nervous mother who, by the look of her, had mothered a great many litters in her time and, though rather plain, was much favoured by the hordes of wild dogs in the neighbourhood. She kept her distance from we people. Her two grown daughters, both much larger than her and rather handsome, were much friendlier. They looked like Alsatians. The family mostly haunted our yard, and sometimes slept under the building when the weather was inclement. They rummaged in the big iron rubbish bin, causing a good deal of mess, and also got thrown scraps by the residents. They knew us all, and were particularly friendly with the children. It was a comfortably symbiotic relationship: in return for food and territory, they generally protected the block from other stray dogs and passing drunks. Russians are great animal lovers and they treated the many stray dogs and cats in the town with kindness or at least tolerance.

I learned later that, from time to time, officials did travel around the town disposing of strays, though I never witnessed this.

Several of our friends had dogs, and they generally preferred large ones. This was slightly comic to me, as Taganrog flats were inclined to be small with very small kitchens. Valya and Genio had a delightful large dog called Geoffrey. If he entered their kitchen whilst one was in there, it was advisable to make one's exit as there wasn't sufficient room for the two of you!

Ina and Vova acquired an extremely tall Afghan hound. Actually, she adopted them. She started turning up outside their ground-floor flat rather regularly and, if the window was open, would stick her head in and gaze at them mournfully. They made a few local enquiries and, as no one appeared to own her, they took her in. She was gentle and extremely independent. They named her Sonya.

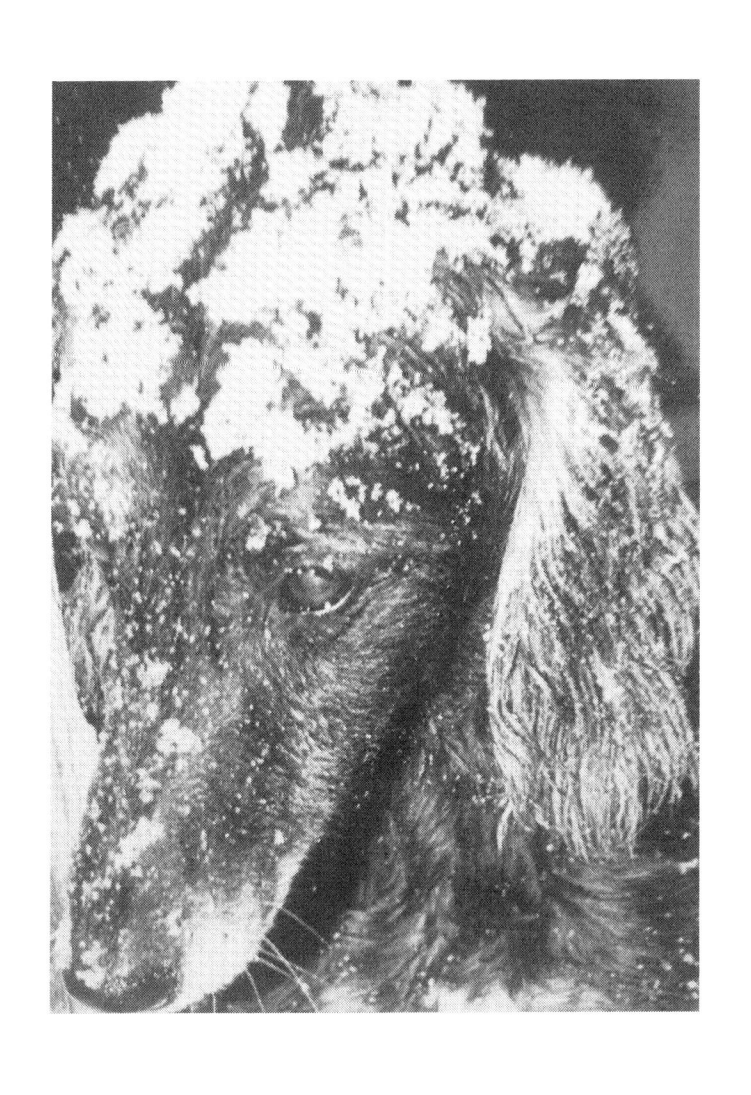

SONYA LOOKING HOPEFUL

In February the two Alsatian daughters on our block were on heat and were pursued relentlessly by a growing horde of dogs. The more handsome of the two, of whom I was particularly fond, got extremely fed up with all the incessant attention, and protected herself by sitting very firmly on her bottom, shrieking and snapping the while. The males were so insistent, and so numerous, that it was only a matter of time before she became impregnated. I suspected she was a virgin.

One night I was kept awake for hours by a gang of stray dogs fighting and yowling just below my window. I eventually went out on the balcony: there were 29 dogs milling about – I counted them. And all for the young bitches. Talk about a gang bang! I filled two 5-litre plastic bottles with water and hurled the water into the doggy fray. It did the trick, at least for long enough for me to get some sleep.

Sometime later I noticed that one of the sisters – the more handsome one – hadn't been around for a while. At first I thought that maybe she had moved away to escape the attentions of all the dogs.

I mentioned this to Paul who agreed that he hadn't seen her either.

The following Monday we discovered her. We had to cross a tram track on our way to school, and we found her corpse in two neat halves just by the further track. I suspect she had found something tasty on the nearer rail, leapt off at the last possible moment to avoid an oncoming tram, not realizing that another tram was approaching on the further rail.

Judging from her expression, she had been killed instantly. Her rather substantial corpse was not removed for a further four days.

Both Paul and I found the experience upsetting, though this would mean there would be more food for her sister and mother – who was expecting again.

At the end of February the old bitch had three delightful, chubby puppies. She must have been hiding them under the building as they were quite well-grown. The kids loved them, though they did make rather a noise at night. Two of them disappeared after a short while, and I learned that one of the male residents had drowned the puppies. He had taken it on himself to keep 'our' dogs to a manageable number, which I guess was sensible.

My teenage student Olya was very keen on dogs, and the family had three, as well as cats. Olya trained the dogs and, in later life, became a professional dog trainer. As she fairly regularly accompanied her mother to St

Petersburg, she sometimes asked me to dog-sit the smallest dog, Roni, to spare her father somewhat, as he had a dicky heart.

In May of my final year in Taganrog, she asked me whether I could look after Roni for a week, and I acquiesced. I missed my own dog, who was in England with my ex-husband, and looked forward to being a dog owner for a while. I would take her for a morning walk before school, and a shorter one at night when school had finished.

One night, I took the little terrier for a long walk by the sea. She was thrilled. I don't think she often walked near the sea as her family lived inland.

The rain had stopped and the air was fresh and clear. The brighter constellations were visible for the first time in quite a while, and Venus and Mars were stunningly bright. I was delighted to see a brand new moon very low in the sky – a slim orange crescent with the dark plane of the full circle faintly visible. The tide was high – higher, I think, than I'd ever seen it. The hideous concrete block where I usually left my jacket, socks and trainers before my barefoot run, normally just licked by the sea, was way out, looking like a half-sunken ship.

Having to walk Roni was a good excuse to explore. One day I took her down a long street where I had not ventured before. It was mostly old bungalows ('old' in Taganrog usually meant a hundred years or so) with lots of trees and shrubs. At one point I came across a tall, very new brick wall into which were set two enormous ornate steel garage doors. This was unusual and I was curious to get a look over the wall. By dint of ferreting around, with Roni at my heels, I got a view of the upper part of the house. It was a sort of gothic 'castle' with white crenellations and one tall, round tower topped by a shiny coned metal roof, on the apex of which rose a splendid shiny wind vane that looked like silver. Best of all were the drainpipes – one either side of the house.

They were gleamingly silvery and each one was capped with a silver crown. This, I thought, had to be the property of what was known as a New Russian.

There were loads of jokes about these New Russians – people who had recently come into a lot of money, by fair means or foul, and liked to demonstrate their wealth. These jokes somewhat resembled the Essex Man and Woman jokes which used to be so common in England.

With the collapse of Communism there was a growing number of nouveau riche, and new showy homes were sprouting up round the suburbs of Taganrog. They reminded me a little of a tiny town called San Gimignano, near Florence, which boasts about thirty stone towers, each taller than the last, built by the 'New Tuscans' of the fifteenth century. People don't change much, do they?

Another morning I rose early and took Roni for a two-hour walk and run along the beach. There was a fierce black sky and the tide was well down. The water was choppy and there were only one or two brave fishing boats silhouetted against the blue-black horizon. An occasional beam of light through a rent in the clouds streaked the sea with silver. Roni was very playful so I threw a stick into a large patch of sea grass, not realising that there were a couple of burdock plants in there.

She emerged with more than twenty burrs hopelessly tangled in her long, woolly coat. Oh dear!

I managed to pick out those that were in danger of hurting her paws, and then had to spend an hour at home patiently unwinding her fur from each spiny seed head. She didn't like this much, especially round her muzzle, so

I rewarded her for her stoicism with some slices of sausage.

The next day I awoke with a terrible migraine and couldn't bring myself to move at all. However, Roni had different ideas. After tail wags, nosings, grunts, whines and short barks, she eventually jumped on top of me and licked my face nearly raw. I tottered out to the yard in my nightdress and propped up a wall, urging her to do her business promptly. I was just about to crawl back inside when I heard a melodic bird song that I couldn't identify. I peered up into a large, broadleaved walnut tree and saw a magnificent pair of golden orioles. I had only once seen this bird before, in the Dordogne, and here they were in urban Taganrog, performing their after-rain concert. I gave Roni a big hug – when I could catch her. I missed her when she was collected the next day.

17 Education

I didn't discover much about secondary schools as I knew very few teenagers, apart from those in my smallish first class. What I did discover, about education in general, is that many parents took it extremely seriously. They would go to great lengths to ensure that their children achieved good marks, and it was the norm to offer bribes to ensure that good marks were given. I had more than one experience of teenagers handing me an envelope from parents containing money just before examinations. In each case, I thanked the students in question and asked them to return it. It was very kind of their parents but I was paid a salary and did not need additional payment. I occasionally came across cases of cheating and made it clear from the first that it was not allowed in my classes. I also pointed out that cheating did not really help the offender. I was particularly interested in one case during my final year in Taganrog. An imaginative and delightful teenager handed me his exercise book to show me a song lyric he had written: it was very good. Unfortunately, I noticed on the opposite page a list of answers to the oral test he would take the following week. I asked him where he'd got them and he shrugged and said it was work he had done for Valya.

Later I spoke to him and his mother, both of whom were mortified, and his mum assured me that it was the only material from the exam he had seen. Valya told me she had also spoken to them both and had told the boy, "You can cheat with Russian teachers, but you can't cheat with English teachers. Remember that."

Russian teachers and students were often in complicity: the teacher allowed the pupil to cheat to ensure that he/she got the required grades. Exam marks were so highly prized that all those involved (pupils, parents, teachers) worked together, and teachers would be punished if their pupils failed to get good marks. It was not uncommon for mothers to cry if their child came home with 'bad' marks – and 'bad' was anything less than five, which was the highest mark. It was a vicious circle. This fact was so well-known that certificates and diplomas acquired in Russia were of little value in other parts of the world.

This saddened me as I personally knew some excellent and dedicated Russian teachers, and, in general, I found that my students were intelligent, well-educated and extremely hard working.

One student, Roman who at that time was a tax collector, confessed that the English classes cost most of his salary. When I asked him whether he considered the classes too expensive, however, he firmly denied this.

I've always believed that education should be enjoyable and stimulating, as motivation is an important ingredient in the learning process. I introduced my students to all sorts of games and activities, whatever their ages, and they responded positively.

However, I found that any activity that only really worked if the individual students competed with one another was not successful. I tried a version of that popular radio show 'Just a Minute' with my adult students, but they would not challenge one another.

I'm personally averse to too much competition as I believe it can lead to selfishness and even duplicity, but I did wonder whether my students' attitude to competition was in part due to their need to support and protect one another in a country which had a particularly uncaring government and bureaucracy.

Certainly, I was delighted by the way they usually helped one another and the generosity they showed in praising and exulting in their fellow students' successes.

It's also interesting that even a game like chess – which one would think of as a highly competitive game and which is very popular in Russia – becomes more of a community sport there. I often witnessed people playing chess outside cafes and in parks and squares and, more often than not, a crowd of bystanders would surround the two players and join in with advice and suggestions.

I kept a file of copies of students' work that particularly appealed to me. One cheeky teenager, Genio, wrote:

'I rite because my teacher said. She made me to rite. Now I have ritten just 95 words but I need 120-80 words. I tink my teacher won't count.'

Actually, his essay totalled 137 words!

I had some original and refreshing results when I gave one class an exercise where they had to write a story using ten or more words from a list I gave them of thirty totally unconnected words. Here are some examples:

'When I write this text I take a pencil in my right hand, but I know that many foreign people writes by left hand. I don't know why! But it is a fact. I think President Bill Clinton writes left hand also…'

'In the 17th century people was rested than now. They ate potato, fish, vegetables and other god food. But some of them was crazy. They believed in human flight, alien races, and other unusual things. They dropped revolution ideas in progressive wind of all Earth.'

'You must not wait if you have an idea. The idea may be crazy, but, believe me, doors are open for everybody. For instance, you want to catch fish. Take a pencil and write it down. Then you need to find one (or a few) fools. A fool can borrow money for your ideas, because he is ready to pay.'

I also read some very amusing Do's and Don'ts. One piece of advice for tourists to Russia was:

'Fly by aeroplane, or by Aeroflot'.

Or how about these Do's and Don'ts for dinner rules?

Wash your hands before a dinner.
Sit down at the table after woman only.
Take the fork in left hand and the knife in right hand.
Don't read, watch TV, sing and dance when you are eating.
Be careful when you are eating fish.
Don't mix some vodka with some beer.
Eat only from YOUR plate.
Don't use clothes of your neighbour and a table cloth instead of a napkin.
Don't worry if your neighbour upset a hot sauce on your suite.
Always remember! You must come back home to your wife.
Have a nice dinner!

Lena gave me information about Russian universities. Most degrees take five years and students start at age 16/17. Up to age 35 a student could get a year's grant of about six million roubles. For the first two years students study ten to eleven subjects, then for three years seven to eight subjects, majoring in four to five.

Exams are twice yearly. The final exams consist of three parts:

1) A 50-page thesis on the Major subjects;

2) A 15-page essay on Ergonomics and the Environment;

3) A 15-page essay on Economics.

All these papers are first checked and marked, with comments, by their 'leader', and then by someone from outside. The overall marks are 3-5, 5 being the highest.

The students have to present these papers. First, they prepare posters or display cards on all three topics, which are displayed in advance. The examiners, who will include some people who are not members of the university staff, listen to a student's presentation for about 15 minutes, and then ask questions. The student also has to demonstrate any practical results, if these are relevant and available. Finally, the comments on the student's work from the leader and the other marker will be read out.

If a student fails his main project, he is out on his ear, but if he fails any of the subsidiary subjects he can retake them later. Whatever the strengths and weaknesses of the Russian educational system, I found students were generally very well informed about their own culture.

They knew their poets, writers, artists and musicians far better than most Brits, and were often surprisingly knowledgeable about English writers too. They were also impressively schooled in mathematics and the sciences. Where they were weaker was in general knowledge about other parts of the world though, with the rapid advance in digital technology, this was becoming less pronounced.

In 1999 I had a small late class of seven male adults, all in their fifties or sixties. They were all engineers and managers from the aeronautics factory, apart from one academic from the university.

The latter, Vladimir, became a good friend of mine as we discovered we lived just round the corner from one another, and walked home together after the class. He was a cultured, kind and gentle soul, and I'm sure was an excellent and much loved teacher. In one session, I happened to make some reference to the Russian author, Mikhael Sholokhov. A moment later, Vladimir and one engineer were on their feet, fists and jaws clenched, yelling at one another in Russian. They were arguing so vociferously that I had trouble making sense of their words. After a stunned moment, I used my best 'strict teacher' voice:

"Gentlemen, please. Would you kindly sit down and behave yourselves. This is an English lesson, not a football match." The two men turned to look at me and then, rather shamefaced, sank back onto their seats.

On the walk home I asked Vladimir what that had been about. It transpired that the engineer had muttered that the books were not actually written by Sholokhov, who was 'a complete fraud'. Vladimir had indignantly defended the author's verity and talent. The interesting point to me was how enraged gentle Vladimir was.

Over the three years that I taught in Taganrog, I quite often received requests from local teachers to sit in on my classes. I was always happy to accommodate them, and to give them photocopies of any materials they liked. Many of the school textbooks for English were terribly out of date and frankly inaccurate. A language is in a constant state of change and books should be regularly updated, which was not happening. I was generally impressed by the teachers I met in this way. They were very keen and open-minded and ready to experiment with new ideas. It was always interesting to compare notes and discuss teaching methods.

18 The Holiday that Wasn't

We had a week's holiday coming up in March. The weather had turned from winter to hot summer with no spring in between. Indeed, the spring plants withered in the heat. So I decided to spend a few days on the Black Sea. I consulted Sergei, the Director of the Day School, as I knew he was familiar with the area. He said he could help me to find somewhere to stay for free, as it was out of season.

A few days on he told me he'd fixed up a flat for me in a place called Chaika (seagull), for which I was immensely grateful. I asked my friend Galya if she would like to accompany me, but she was not able to get time off, so I was resigned to going solo. Sergei gave me the address and instructions on how to get there. I travelled by a train that left Taganrog at 1.25 pm on Sunday and arrived in the town of Tuapse at 3.00 am on the Monday, from where I was to catch a bus to Chaika.

The weather reversed whilst I was rocking on the train, and was freezing in Tuapse.

I eventually found an all-night café in the sleeping town where I took refuge until the departure of my bus at about 7.00. I asked the driver to please tell me when we reached Chaika, but he forgot, so I had a two-hour wait at the end of the bus run before it did the return journey.

Chaika turned out to be a large holiday camp on the sea, and I had trouble locating the correct building. At one time I entered what I thought was going to be the flat, but found myself in a large plush office with a rather surprised official staring at me across a vast desk. After a somewhat surreal conversation I discovered I was in the wrong building.

When I eventually found the right building I was led, not to a flat, but to a small room with a pile of furniture stacked in one corner. It was cold and dank, there was no heating, and the water in the bathroom was turned on in my honour but was cold. Worst of all, the kitchen was a shared one and had no cooking equipment and I discovered there were no shops either. Or none that were open. The pleasant woman in charge of the block helped me move the furniture and supplied me with bedding.

I was so cold and tired by this time that I just dropped into bed fully clothed, but it was too cold to sleep. I sat up and pondered what to do. I had noticed on the bus ride that the hotels and restaurants we passed all appeared to be closed, or were in process of being re-roofed and repainted in preparation for the summer.

I hunted for the woman in charge – there seemed to be no one around – and eventually located her in a tiny room with a heater – oh joy! She kindly gave me a mug of steaming tea, and didn't seem the slightest bit surprised when I told her I had decided to return to Taganrog. She contacted the on-site minibus driver who offered to drive me to the bus stop for Tuapse as the rain was torrential by this time. Really, the skeleton staff could not have been more helpful and kind, though they obviously thought I was quite mad to visit out of season.

In Tuapse, the next train wasn't due for three hours, so back I trailed to the same café until half an hour before departure, when I made a dash through the downpour to the station. I thought at first, with sinking heart, that the station building was closed too, as

"I NEVER LEARN, DO I? "

there was no sign of light or life. When I saw a man race up a flight of stone steps and disappear through a huge double door that I had assumed was locked, I followed him.

It was pitch dark. I came to a halt just inside, allowing my eyes to adjust to the dark, and only then realised that this was in fact the waiting room and that there were quite a lot of people sitting silently on benches. I shuffled cautiously through the gloom until I located a space at the farther end. Was there a power cut?

After about twenty minutes I heard a sharp tapping sound, and gradually made out a tall, bearded man who was limping towards me with a stick. I was preparing to make room for him on the bench, but he tottered past me and then began to stretch upwards, waving his stick wildly in the air and sort of poking it from time to time at the wall. I was intrigued. What was he doing? Was he mad? A moment later the waiting room was positively flooded with light. Only then did I realise that he had been trying to reach a light switch placed very high on the wall!

When the train pulled in, I sank thankfully onto my couchette bunk and slept for about twelve hours. That was by far the shortest holiday I have ever experienced, and the most uncomfortable, but what on earth did

I expect, given that it was free, at the end of March, and in Russia!

19 Difficult Days

Three weeks later something rather odd occurred. A stranger knocked on our flat door and asked us when we were leaving the flat. We told her that the school had paid up to September. The woman, so far as we could understand, expected us to leave at the end of April and it was then the 20th. Paul and I suspected that our terrible landlady was just trying something on. On the last day of April the mystery of this stranger was revealed. It transpired that our landlady was even more of a crook than we had thought for she didn't own the flat at all. It actually belonged to a family who had been living in Moscow and she was simply a neighbour who had offered to take care of the flat in their absence. The owners had returned to Taganrog to sell the flat, having no idea that there were tenants in it. They would understandably have liked us to leave immediately but, being decent souls, and realising that it was not our fault, they agreed to hang on for a while until we found somewhere else.

Our contract stipulated that the school would supply our accommodation, but Paul and I no longer trusted Anya's choices, so we S.O.S.ed our students to help us locate somewhere suitable. However, before we had a chance to view any properties, Anya told us we were moving to another flat the next day.

We frantically packed our growing accumulation of possessions, whilst our horror 'landlady' arrived with three burly men who proceeded to remove absolutely everything in the flat, including light fittings and curtain rails! Did the owners know about this, I wondered?

The old day school bus, with all seats removed, turned up with a contingent of male teachers from the day school, courtesy of Sergei, who saved the day once again with his kindness. They drove us to the new location and helped us move in. We could not believe what we found and I could see the teachers were shocked and embarrassed on our account.

The tiny bathroom contained a toilet that didn't flush, a badly cracked small basin, and a shower with such feeble water pressure that it barely trickled. This was probably just as well, as the flexes for the water heater dangled at my eye level right across and under the shower head.

There were two bedrooms but no doors in the doorways, and one wardrobe which had neither hanging rail nor hooks and two shelves which were dangling from one screw apiece. The beds were so lumpy that the three of us preferred to sleep on the floor!

The living room had one electric point that worked, so we had to heap our kettle, cassette players, CD players and toaster on the floor beside it and there was no kitchen at all. Just a fridge one side of the front door, and a gas cooker the other, with no cupboards or work space.

A few hours after we had moved in, Anya turned up bearing two plastic bowls. An odd gift, one might think, though given the state of the basin and the fact there was no sink, it was decidedly practical! She beamed at me, saying, "Isn't it nice! So central," and was surprised when I told her that the flat was totally unacceptable and we were going to look for another one. She offered to cancel our classes that evening, to which we heartily agreed. The word had got around. A contingent of our students arrived to wish us well. Their reactions were interesting.

Some of them were mortified, and apologised profusely, while others took one look and collapsed with laughter. However, they all agreed that we could not possibly stay there.

Later that evening, Roman, who had a lightness of touch and an irrepressible sense of humour, arrived with a bag of beer. When he eventually rose to leave, we discovered that the door to the outside landing had locked itself, and we could not open it. Eventually, I climbed out of a front window, which involved a great leap from the sill as there was a deep well between the outer wall and the pavement. I tried to open the door from the outside, with no success. Finally, Roman tore the lock out of the wall with the aid of my one screwdriver and a section of wood from one of the broken chairs! The next day, on Roman's advice, we took all our computers to the basement of a business belonging to a friend of his for safekeeping.

I learned from one of the day teachers that Sergei and Anya had a flaming row the day after we moved. The male teachers had told him about the state of the flat and he accused Anya of being stupid and irresponsible. Everyone was on edge.

One of my advanced students, Tolik, offered to help us find a more suitable flat. He was an interesting guy, who spoke fluent English and had made a lot of money in business before losing much of it. He was blond and fair-skinned and sometimes declared that he was not Russian at all.

He might have been part Greek though his family name suggested Tartar origins. His maternal grandfather was a diplomat and, when Tolik was a small boy and his mother separated from his father, he lived with his grandparents in Afghanistan for a time. He was there when the Russians first invaded, and the President was killed, and this had left a permanent scar. He told me he loved the Afghan President and could not understand why, suddenly, he was apparently 'bad'. Like several Russians I knew, he would slate his country and declare he would leave at the first opportunity, yet he was also patriotic in many ways.

Our friends Ina and Vova, who lived in a student hostel, invited us to supper to watch a video of Jane Eyre. It should have been a good evening, but both Paul and I were tense and exhausted.

When Paul made some arrogant Virgoan remark to me, I emptied my glass of white wine over his head. He promptly retaliated by tipping his much larger glassful over mine! Vova was deeply shocked and reprimanded Paul severely. "Never," he said, "never do that to a lady!" To which Paul shirtily replied that I had started it, which was of course true.

I sat cross-legged and stonily silent for a moment, then stood up, made my apologies to Ina and Vova for my infantile behaviour, and said I was going for a walk to calm down.

I stalked tearfully down to the port. It was nearly midnight. There was a bright moon, lots of stars, and a rather wild sea. I realised that I hadn't had a moment to myself, or the chance of a walk, for at least a fortnight, and began slowly to unwind. It was very hot, even at that hour, and the sea looked tempting. I climbed down the embankment, stripped off, and had a long and glorious swim. But when I clambered ashore, I could not find my clothes.

Quite a lot of people were strolling along the promenade above, while I crawled unsteadily – and horribly naked – over the rocks below, searching desperately for my clothes.

After about an hour, I sat disconsolately on a rock, my arms wound round my knees for warmth, and faced the possibility that I would have to wait for dawn. I also gloomily considered the possibility that a cruising police car might spot me, and imagined the next day's headlines.

As I sat thus, gazing out to sea, I noticed that the waves were driving at a very sharp leftward angle to the shore and it dawned on me that I might have climbed ashore much further to the left than I had thought.

I was correct about that, and did eventually find my clothes. When I let myself into the flat, Paul was still up. He had been very worried about me and was therefore angry. I apologised, he did likewise, and we made our peace and crawled to our hard-floor beds.

Dear Tolik did indeed find us a decent flat, which was spacious, doored, well-furnished, clean, and in a nice area near the main beach. The water heater needed replacing, and the owners – a retired couple called Zoya and Alexandr – promised to fix it promptly. We would move there in a couple of days.

20 The Wedding

Paul and Lena had decided to get married in Russia, before returning to the UK. I suggested to Lena, who was very active and inclined to be adventurous, that I stood her a horse ride as a wedding present, and she jumped at the offer. She had once sat on a horse as a little girl. To make it more fun, I also invited my student Galya, a beautiful, lively Ukrainian lawyer, who had never ridden before. I warned both girls that it would be wise to wear two pairs of trousers plus boots to protect their inner thighs and calves, but of course they ignored my advice. Would that look elegant?

From the stable, we walked the horses through the town to the park. The two Russian girls who accompanied us were incredibly laid back, considering all the traffic and two absolute beginners, and later admitted that this was a 'first': they usually only rode in the park or travelled right out of town with horseboxes. No wonder we attracted a lot of attention.

When we got down to the wood alongside the main beach you could sense the horses' excitement. We had a canter along a dirt track. My horse suddenly shied and I flew over her head and crashed to the hard sun-baked ground.

None of us were wearing hard hats. I rather shakily pulled myself upright, caught the horse, and remounted. I had been very lucky. A lot of poplars had recently been felled and there were many short, sharp trunk bases, but fortunately I landed on grass and weeds.

Later, Lena and Galya tried a few little jumps, brave foolish girls. We were out for over two hours and both girls clearly thoroughly enjoyed the experience. Unlike we Brits, who frankly take health and safety to ridiculous lengths sometimes, there was very little consideration of that kind in Taganrog Over the next few days, Galya, Lena and I regularly compared injuries. My spine was so severely bruised that I had to sleep on a mattress on the floor. My whole pelvic girdle seemed to have seized up so I suffered constipation as well. I was sucking arnica tablets like some people suck polo mints. Lena had multi-coloured bruises on both inner thighs and looked like an abstract painting. Galya couldn't sit down for several days and hobbled rather than walked. Was it, I asked myself, really an appropriate wedding gift?

As the wedding drew nearer, I started gathering Russian wedding traditions. On the wedding day, the groom must 'buy' the bride by negotiating a sum of money with the bride's representative. He will not be allowed to see her in her finery until the money has changed hands and his best man will conduct negotiations on his behalf. While this is going on, the entranceway to the bride's home is blocked by a strip of tape closely guarded by old women.

The groom must identify the lipstick imprint of his wife to be on an apple, a napkin, or a piece of cloth. This will have been stamped with many different women's lips. He might also have to pick out the bride from a group of veiled ladies. He will be questioned by the bride's family, and woe betide him if he does not know the birth date of his future mother-in-law!

The wedding was on Saturday, 6th June, and it was incredibly hot. Paul, Viktor, his best man, and I drove over to the little flat of Lena's bridesmaid, Lilia, in the afternoon. Lena's Mum was decorating the bonnet of a car with flowers under a net and I tried, rather ineptly, to help. A crowd of old women and children had gathered near the front door. As we approached, two fearsome, toothless old women – neighbours I think – barred the door, across which a length of ribbon had been tied. Then Lena's twin sister came out and started haggling with Viktor over the bride price. She had a rather good job in a bank and was a tough bargainer. Viktor didn't stand a chance! Eventually, a price was agreed, Paul paid up, and everybody cheered. Only then were we allowed into the building. After a glass of champagne, tea and a few itsy bitsies, we all drove to the marriage bureau. The ceremony took all of ten to fifteen minutes, and was a conveyer belt process. We trooped in one door, stood around in an awkward huddle, and then were ushered out the other door as the next happy couple-to-be traipsed in.

We then piled into various cars and drove to Peter the Great's statue above the port. It's a Russian tradition for just-marrieds to visit the major statues in their town and one will often see a number of white-gowned brides with groom and guests fluttering round well-known statues and posing for photos. Fortunately, Paul and Lena were content with just the one statue, as the town boasted many. From there we drove to Nadia's Nightclub for the reception. Lena and family certainly hadn't stinted: the tables were groaning with food and every kind of drink.

It took a while for the party to get going as the back room had no windows or air conditioning and everyone was dripping with heat. However, as the alcohol flowed and the evening became cooler, people began to unwind, and there was lively dancing, a good deal of kissing and cuddling, and some idiotic games.

On the following Sunday, Lena had booked a bus to take about thirty people to a lake in the countryside. We all straggled along a path by the lake with bags of food and drink. We passed a group of picnickers some way off the path who had a dog tied to a tree. The dog was barking, and I barked back. What an inane thing to do!

The next thing I knew, the dog was haring towards me, his lead dangling, teeth bared and snarling. I stood stock still and prayed he would stop short. This might just have worked, if Vova had not leaped in front of me and beaten the dog on the snout. Everyone was yelling at the owners, the owners were yelling back, but the dog was finally retrieved and tied more firmly to that tree. Normality was restored in a twinkling. It was only several minutes later that I realised Vova's hand was bleeding badly. It bore several tooth marks. He had made no sound and I felt inexplicably angry (shame, no doubt) that he was so heroic. He eventually agreed to let me pour a good deal of high alcohol vodka over the wound and I am glad to say that his hand healed well with no problems. Never again would I mimic a dog!

From then on, it was an enjoyable and lazy day, with a delicious barbecue, swimming in the cool water, and dozing under the trees.

Early in June Anya had told Paul that he would have to leave by the end of June as several students were dropping out, because of the summer break and other commitments. He was upset about this as he and Lena had applied for Lena's visa to the UK and needed to stay in Russia until the visa was sorted. They could not afford to remain without Paul's salary. Jonathan had acquired a very nice Russian girlfriend and was in no hurry to leave.

I, on the other hand, was perfectly happy to return early to England. I had a home to go to as my tenants had left a few weeks previously, I did not enjoy the intense heat, and was eager to see my family again. I suggested that we hold a meeting to discuss potential plans and offered to leave by mid-June provided suitable arrangements could be made for my students. We compared our registers

THE WEDDING PICNIC

and worked out how we could combine my classes with theirs. We then asked Anya for a meeting and she agreed to our ideas.

When I told my students our decision there were a couple of days of 'deputations' and sulks, but they came round. I actually felt it would do them good to have a change: they had become rather too comfortable and a bit lazy.

Before I left, I agreed to return for a third year and Jonathan was also contracted. It would be strange not to have Paul around, and I would miss Lena too. But I looked forward to another stint.

21 Hard Times

While I was back with my family in England, Russia suffered an economic crisis; the rouble had gone through the floor. I wondered whether it was crazy to return there in September. Yet the fact was I felt committed to that little school in Taganrog, which had offered me the opportunity to learn to teach and had welcomed me with open arms, and I had made some good friends there as well. So I decided to return come what may.

I arrived in Moscow's Kazanskaya Station on 11th September. The facilities had greatly improved in the two months I had been away: more waiting rooms, chairs, shops and eating places, and it was humming with activity. Long, packed trains were coming and going, each flaunting their personal names: the 'Tatarstan' to Kazan and the 'Giguli' to Samara.

A very smart and imperious young woman with two hassled men in tow was trying to get an enormous amount of luggage onto the Samara train: she had obviously been on a mega shopping spree. She tried one carriage after another, and each time, the stewardess gave her a flea in her ear and refused her entry.

Her beautiful heavily made-up face was getting pinker and pinker and her wide mouth sulkier and sulkier, while the men tried to placate her. She started unpacking several of the huge cardboard boxes and tried to transfer their contents to large plastic bags, which inevitably split and ripped.

Then she marched off to the further end of the train with one of her escorts, leaving the other to guard her boxes. He looked relieved for the break and thankfully lit up!

Eventually, the girl plus escort returned. She looked furious. I suspect she was told she would have to put everything in the luggage van, probably at considerable expense.

I enjoyed watching this drama unfold as I waited for the 'Tikki Don' to leave.

I had a first class compartment, courtesy of Language Link – was this promotion? My companion for the journey was a pleasant Armenian who was working as a maths and physics teacher in Baku on the Caspian Sea. When I asked him about the economic situation he said that he thought things would return to normal eventually; that the Communists would not return to power, and that Yeltsin would undoubtedly be OUT.

My first day back in Taganrog was being talked about by my students before I left the previous June, for it was the three hundredth anniversary of the founding of the town by Peter the Great.

Wandering around, I immediately noticed certain physical changes for the better. In the town centre, several of the potholed pavements had been re-laid; there were many more street lights – rather handsome ones. An imposing new statue of Tsar Alexander II, astride a vicious-looking eagle, took centre stage in Bankovskaya Square.

I strolled down the Old Steps to the main beach, then hesitated, momentarily confused. Gone was the wood and straggly bushes where I had my riding accident; gone the weaving sandy paths busy with ants. Instead there were neat coloured brick paths, radiating out from a central plinth of shiny black stone, which bore an inscription commemorating 300 years of the city. The poplar trees that remained were in neat regulated lines, and there were lots of smart new benches, iron rubbish bins shaped like tulips and more handsome lamps. I couldn't help feeling a slight sense of loss for the one-time wild stretch.

Everywhere, in shop windows, on banners strung across the streets and on people's front gates were the words 'TAGANROG 300 YEARS'. But even as the streets began to fill with people, dressed in their bright festive best, I felt that the atmosphere was somewhat muted.

There was not that bubbling gaiety I remembered. Perhaps this was just the effect of jet lag, but I returned to my flat feeling somewhat deflated.

The next day, Sunday, Anya, her assistant Olga and Sergei all popped in, bringing goodies and a sack of potatoes from a relative's dacha. It was good to see them again. I asked them whether the school would be affected by the economic crisis, and Anya admitted that there were only half as many students, as many could no longer afford the fees. However, some new students were beginning to trickle in, nearly all businessmen from the aeroplane plant.

In the following days I talked to several friends about the economic downturn. Very few of them had lost money directly because, since the crash in 1994 when many people lost all their savings, most Russians no longer kept their money in banks.

But of course it was already affecting job availability and salaries, which were worth half what they were. Most prices, at least of local products, were stable, but foreign goods were either much more expensive or unavailable because shopkeepers were stockpiling them. I am not much of an economist and don't really understand the behaviour of money, but I suspected that if Jonathan and I were paid in roubles valued against the dollar, as previously, the school would soon go bust and have to close. I therefore suggested to him that we offered to receive roubles valued at ten to the dollar, whatever the circumstances, and Jonathan agreed. Although this meant that our salaries would be ridiculously low by West European standards, we would still have enough to live on, and this proved to be the case.

Returning from school one night, I noticed that the new statue of Alexander II was partly screened under quite a pile of red roses and carnations, and I wondered why. I asked my students about this and they told me it had been commissioned by the town council in honour of the 300th anniversary. It is apparently an exact replica of a statue that was destroyed in the Revolution. Some townspeople were annoyed about it, as it cost a lot of money that they felt could have been better spent but, if the flowers were anything to go by, not everybody felt that way. I, too, felt annoyed that – if they had to erect yet another statue – why not create an adventurous new one rather than replicating the old style. When Ina and Vova dropped by later, I told them this. Vova smiled rather lop-sidedly. "I know, Gilli," he said. "I hate my country too. I vould sell it tomorrow but I don't sink anyone vould buy it." Actually, Vova was intensely loyal to his country, but he had no illusions either.

One of the aspects I love about my Russian friends is their sense of humour. They have more jokes about themselves and their politicians than we have. Roman told me a good joke about trains. Under Lenin, when a train broke down, everyone disembarked and worked hard to repair it. Under Stalin, when a train broke down the driver was shot and the passengers were removed at gunpoint and ordered to repair it. Under Kruschev, the passengers got out and patiently listened to a very long speech encouraging them to rebuild the train so that it was back in service within ten years. Under Brezhnev, when the train broke down, two passengers were told to stand either side of the train and shake it about so that it appeared to be moving. We then discussed how we could extend the joke to include Yeltsin, and decided that all the passengers would have been asked to empty their pockets to provide funds for repairs, which would be repaid at good interest: but by the time the interest was repaid – if ever – the rouble would be worth one-tenth of what it had been!

Beneath such jokes, as with much humour, is something rather sad. How many times have I heard a Russian say: "We are trapped in our history."

Sergei and a friend invited me to join them on a crazy driving holiday the following May. They planned to drive from Taganrog, via Moscow, Finland, Denmark and Belgium, to England. Their pilgrimage? To worship the Beatles in the Beatles Museum in Liverpool and to run right round Manchester United's home pitch! "Where would we sleep?" I cautiously asked. "In the car, of course." I decided right then to politely decline, though I would gladly give them what advice or contacts I could.

Despite all the new street lights, the streets seemed rather less well-lit than the previous winter; presumably there were insufficient funds to light them all. I bumped into Ina who was in a rage because she had fallen into a deep hole in the pavement. The hole was covered with fallen autumn leaves which was why she didn't spot it. Her shoulder bag was flooded and, what was worse, the paperback she had been reading was ruined. I suggested, somewhat wryly, that perhaps she should make a complaint. "Complain to who?" replied Ina.

I had had arguments with friends on this topic and had suggested that if more people complained more often, perhaps something would improve, though this was frankly arrogant on my part. The fact is that the ordinary Russian people have always been considered of little account, whether tyrannised by landlords, tsars, invading nomads or Communist officials. They have survived by supporting one another, using their initiative and imagination and being extraordinarily tolerant but, as one wise friend said, when they really get riled these gentle people can 'become like ravening beasts'. And could one blame them?

Revolution Day, on 10th November, was, miraculously, a clear windy day, so I decided to take a long walk. I was thrilled to see about a hundred cranes fishing busily. Taganrog is on their migration route.

In the old fishing village, the fishermen's wives were scrubbing green gunge off the nets, while their husbands lounged about. Quite a few rusting hulks lurched in the harbour, and the sea gave off a lovely tangy scent – a mixture of salty mud, weed and wetness. The last of the autumn leaves littered the pavements and most of the poplars were bare.

22 ALL CHANGE

In mid-November, Anya started saying things to me that made my ears prick up. It started fairly harmlessly. For instance, she casually mentioned that she had met up with the director of our organisation's 'sister school' in Rostov. I was surprised and curious. Why had Language Link never mentioned that they had a school in Rostov? Moreover, she said, if we tied in with this school, we could be directly accountable to Rostov rather than Moscow, which would be much more convenient. I could certainly see the sense in that, as Rostov was only 50 km away. Later, Anya told me that the Rostov school made contracts with teachers direct from London and got all their books from London, too – much more quickly and easily than from Moscow. That sounded odd. When she suggested that I meet up with the Rostov director, I hesitantly agreed. She gave me a name and telephone number.

Before I had a chance to follow this up, I received a call from the director in Moscow, saying that he was sick of Anya's dishonesty and machinations, that none of her figures even remotely added up, and that he was planning to fire her. I suspect that Anya must have got wind of something, for a few days after my call from Moscow, she informed me that the Rostov director was coming to Taganrog with one of his teachers and would like to meet me. Both alarmed and intrigued, I agreed to meet them in my flat.

They arrived as planned: Anya, an elderly Canadian teacher, and a rather smooth-talking young Russian by the name of Sasha. The latter was charming, intelligent and businesslike, but I didn't quite trust him. A few direct questions clarified matters somewhat. He didn't work for a 'sister school' but ran a school in Rostov with his mother. It became evident that he was touting for Jonathan and me, and that Anya was planning to set up on her own, under the aegis of the Rostov school. I told them all that I wasn't interested but that I could not speak for Jonathan.

That evening, Anya wasn't in school. However, she had left 'an important message for us' with her assistant. To wit, that Jonathan and I were in fact working in Russia illegally; that our visas must be renewed on 8th December and would only be granted if we worked, either for the Rostov School, or for the Russian Education Department. Jonathan was extremely alarmed, but I assured him that it was all bluff and that I would phone Moscow after school.

Later the same night, about half an hour after I got home, I received a panic-stricken call from Jonathan. He had received a rather threatening call from a man called Sasha in Rostov, who said that we now worked for his agency and that he would be contacting us soon. I told him not to worry, and spent the next hour or so trying to contact our Moscow director, without success. The following morning, he phoned me back and, after I had filled him in, he said he and his co-director would be flying to Taganrog early the following week, and to 'just hang on in there'.

We got through the next few days somehow, though the atmosphere was murky. I think many of the students were afraid that the school might close and, I must confess, I too feared this might be the result. However, I had been assured by Moscow that the school would continue and I had no reason to disbelieve them.

Both directors duly arrived and began, slowly and patiently, to sort things out. It seemed that Anya had spirited away the entire school funds: the school was bankrupt. We called a meeting for students and parents, whose mass exhalation of relief when they were calmly assured that the school would remain open, was audible. I found it difficult to believe that Anya had deliberately mishandled funds. I was inclined to suspect that she was financially incompetent, got into a dreadful mess, and then tried by whatever desperate means to remain in control and hang onto the school that she was undoubtedly proud to have started.

After a few days the male director returned to Moscow, leaving his co-director, Natasha, to cope. She was a kind woman of great integrity, and displayed remarkable patience as she tried to ascertain the facts. Anya stubbornly refused to co-operate and, with bulldog tenacity, 'sat on' records and files until Natasha gently drew them forth.

She asked me if I knew of anyone who might be a suitable candidate for Anya's job and I immediately thought of Valya. She had been on the spot from day one, supporting Anya, myself and Paul in all sorts of ways. She was an experienced teacher of teachers and had excellent English.

And she was tough, which I suspected was an essential quality – and one that Anya lacked. However, she had a demanding job at the Pedagogical Institute and I did not know whether she would be interested. In fact, she was delighted at the possibility, was interviewed by Natasha, and turned up trumps.

We had considered closing the school for a week or two but, with Valya's energy and enthusiasm, we decided to close for two days only.

When Anya came into the school to go through some papers with Natasha, she looked bent and defeated and my heart went out to her. She had invested heavily in the project but she lacked the necessary skills and discrimination. She had apparently bribed officials by allowing their relatives to attend classes scot-free, and had then overcharged other students to try and balance accounts. It also explained why she had found us such unsuitable accommodation.

Over the next few weeks Valya manfully worked her way through all Anya's paperwork, which was completely unsystematic, with help from her husband, Genio. She discovered that Anya had at least three different accounts: one for the company; one for herself; and one for nobody knew who.

And meanwhile, the economic downturn was continuing to bite. Ten eggs cost double what one paid a week before, and the same went for many other common products. The teachers who worked at the day school had not been paid for three months – and yet they went on working dedicatedly. I learned that the Duma in Moscow was debating whether to make it legal to own land.

I had not realized the fact that all Russian land belonged to the State, at least in theory. The older generation – grandparents – were still very much attached to the land and many had dachas, which somewhat resembled our allotments. At weekends, from spring to autumn, they travelled out of town by bus or train, busily planting and harvesting, and returned laden with produce, to bottle for the winter or sell in the markets. In the towns, too, any waste plot of earth would be cultivated by someone. It was also a popular pastime to gather fungi, berries and any other edible plants wherever one found them. Private ownership would certainly change all that.

In mid-December, several students again expressed anxiety about the possible closure of the school because it was not 'legal'. Further questioning revealed the source of this rumour. It was Anya! Valya was worried that we would lose students if the rumour continued but I told her not to worry. She had never been much liked by most of the students and, if she was planning to start another school, very few would be tempted to switch. This proved to be the case, and we all began to settle down into the new set up.

A RUSSIAN DACHA

23 St Petersburg

The school was on holiday for two weeks in January, so I decided to visit St Petersburg. I had never seen the city and had often been told that it was one of the most beautiful on earth, so I was looking forward to the experience. As usual, dear Language Link was able to offer me the use of a teacher's flat for the week.

My beloved teenage student Olya frequently travelled to St Petersburg with her mother, who was a writer of children's readers and had to deliver her scripts and liaise with her publishers on a fairly regular basis. When Olya heard that I was going to visit, she said she might be able to join me for some of the time. I was delighted and told her I would be happy for her to come if her parents agreed.

For the first three days I was on my own. Wandering round the city, I was reminded of Hans Andersen's The Snow Queen. It was as if she had stroked the place with her chill, loveless hands. The colours of the great buildings were muted by mist and damp and looked stark; the wide avenues formed bitter wind tunnels; the rivers and canals were blocked with grey ice in which were trapped dead frozen ducks and dogs in the midst of discarded trolleys, prams, paper, orange peel, bottles and other detritus.

The golden cupolas had no sun to make them gleam and, worst of all, the Snow Queen had sprinkled ice crystals into the hearts of the people, who looked grey, sullen and silent. It seemed like a mistake to visit the city in winter.

I spent the best part of a day in the Hermitage, which was well worth a visit. I particularly enjoyed the wonderful collection of netsuke, which were housed right at the top of the building. These are miniature Japanese carvings which were used as toggles.

Olya arrived on 4th January, and we celebrated by seeing an excellent production of Tchaikovsky's Mazeppa at the Marinsky Theatre.

The next day we visited the Summer Palace, which was some way out of St Petersburg. It looked beautiful under a recent fall of snow, and it was there that I recalled that the city was very badly bombed in the last war. What I was looking at was a faithful reconstruction of a destroyed city. The palace was still undergoing restoration, all these years later. I bought a plastercast from two plasterers who were working in one of the rooms – very nice men who told me they hadn't been paid for months so were making these models of mouldings to raise a bit of money. Much of the city is a kind of vast, elegant museum – a memorial to a once grand empire. It is all so planned, so perfect, so huge. Like Venice – which I feel bears many resemblances to St P. – I think they are places that should only be visited in good weather. For all that Moscow is crowded, noisy and polluted, I preferred it. It seemed so much more energetic and dynamic, and had a healthier mix of old and new. I might have liked St P. more had I received the occasional smile or friendly remark, but everyone looked so miserable!

Just to add insult to injury, when I bought my return ticket I was charged three times as much as I had paid in Taganrog. When I pointed this out, they asked to see my work permit. Being a public holiday, there was no chance of getting someone from Language Link to provide me with the necessaries, so I just had to fork out. Olya and I bought our tickets together, and I made it perfectly clear to the ticket lady that I did not want to take the train via the Ukraine as I didn't have a Ukrainian visa. I later discovered, quite by chance, that the ticket lady had in fact sold me a ticket via the Ukraine and I spent the next two hours desperately trying to change it, without success. There was no indication on the ticket that it went into the Ukraine, but apparently the ticket number would have made this plain to those in the know.

I eventually phoned the British Consulate to ask whether they thought I'd be OK, but they didn't know. Olya and I decided to risk it. The more fool me: I should have remembered Paul's non-arrival.

Of course, the result was that, when my passport was checked at the first stop in the Ukraine, I was politely requested to get off the train. I told Olya to go on without me, but she loyally insisted on staying with me, for which I was immensely grateful. We were escorted to a dismal police station, where I was eventually interviewed by a large and courteous police officer. After taking down details, he asked me whether I had any complaints. I told him, Yes, I thought the whole business was idiotic, as I was travelling on a Russian train from one Russian city to another on a track which just happened to detour through a small corner of the Ukraine. I had had no intention of leaving the train until I reached Rostov. He eyed me thoughtfully – and somewhat icily – and proceeded to write a long list of something on a pad. When he slid the paper across the table to me, I saw it was a list of about thirty countries. "These" he said, "are the countries for which we have to attain visas." I saw his point. "Complaint withdrawn" I replied. We spent the next six freezing and miserable hours pacing up and down the concrete floor of the police station and my heart went out to little Olya, who was so brave and loyal.

  At about 10.00 pm, we were escorted to a train returning to Moscow. I was informed that my passport would be returned to me by police at Belgorod, just over the Russian border. As we had no tickets, we were summarily dumped in a corridor plus luggage, where we got in everybody's way. I was in a silent rage by this time and, when the train drew into another station and yet more Ukrainian police boarded the train and asked to see my passport, I surlily ignored them. One burly chap jabbed me in the back. I spun round, spat out that I didn't have a passport and, if he wanted to know why, ask THEM: I jabbed my finger towards the stewardess in the corridor and then, for good measure, cuffed him twice on the shoulder. His jaw dropped open in astonishment and he meekly plodded off to speak to her! Looking back now, I marvel at my arrogance.

Shortly after this, the very nice stewardess from the next carriage (the word must have got around) came up to us and suggested that we sit in one of her empty compartments, which we gratefully did. We were due to reach Belgorod about 11.30 pm and I checked it out in my Lonely Planet Guide. It sounded like the absolute pits – not the ideal place to spend the night. So Olya and I agreed that the best thing to do was to organise a quiet deal with the stewardess. In return for a few hundred roubles, she let us sleep in the couchette, on the understanding that if paying travellers boarded the train in the night, we might have to move to her own compartment. Fortunately, this didn't happen, and Olya was soon fast asleep.

I looked affectionately at her blonde-haired, slight sleeping form and silently thanked her for her loyalty and calm support. I recalled Paul's unfortunate non-arrival and chided myself for my stupidity. Had I not been so impetuous and impatient, I would not have landed myself – and a sweet and innocent teenager – in this situation. "Gilli," I whispered inwardly. "One day you are going to curse the wrong official and find yourself in serious trouble. Less arrogance and more good sense, my girl!"

We drew into Kazanskaya Station at seven in the morning, bought two singles to Rostov, and then had to hang around for fourteen hours. We pooled our remaining roubles and had just enough to buy bottled water and some bananas. The station was packed and many patient families with young children had to wait ages for their connection, just like us. Some had already travelled from as far away as Tashkent or places near the Chinese border. Very few people had books, newspapers or simple games for their children. As Olya and I played dot to dot, battleships and cruisers, and various drawing games to pass the time, I could see people watching us with growing curiosity and interest.

Russians strike me as being incredibly patient: waiting seems to be built into their psyche.

The journey to Rostov was blissfully uneventful. Olya and I were both exhausted and spent most of the time dozing on our bunks. Altogether, we had spent three days and nights on trains, in railway stations or in police stations. What would I have done without little Olya, bless her little – probably rather smelly by this time – woollen socks!

Returning to Taganrog, I immediately noticed the difference. The people looked much healthier, browner and not pallid. Their eyes were brighter, their movements more vigorous, and they were noticeably more talkative. There was a distinct difference, it seemed to me, between the Russians of the north and those of the south.

I slipped Olya's return fare to Rostov in an envelope, with a note, and gave it to her parents, Olga and Vassily. After all, I was the visa-less one, not Olya, and she need not have left the train at Kharkov. They would not accept the money. I had to be satisfied with a present for Olya, and the offer of some free English lessons, which were accepted.

24 THE ECONOMIC CRISIS BITES

By mid-January many teachers in the area were threatening to strike. Our Taganrog teachers had not been paid for several months. Teachers in Rostov had been paid – in a manner of speaking – in ventilators! Presumably a local factory had a stock of them and no buyers, for who wants ventilators when it's -10^0C? There was a better story: apparently, in one region, teachers were offered free coffins in lieu of payment. I could not verify this.

What interested me most about these stories was that, though naturally indignant, the teachers did not in fact strike – at least in Taganrog. Before coming to Russia, I had a picture of the 'typical' Russian being a large, rather aggressive person. Well, large some of them certainly are (though in the south obesity was rare), but aggressive, no. Generally, I found them to be soft-spoken, gentle people, far less aggressive, I would say, than your average Brit.

The twentieth of February was traditionally celebrated as the end of winter, when people make pancakes. It was still wintry on that day, but the next morning was, indeed, a pleasantly warm and sunny one, the first time in the year I dared venture out without a warm hat. The sea ice had gone, but for a few little icebergs further out. There was still a fair bit of ice along the shore, of varying textures. Some were paper-thin and delicately traced; some were thicker slabs with sticklike patterns engraved in them; yet others were thicker chunks, looking like the skin of a sick old person covered in boils and scabs (possibly frozen sea-surface froth). Then there were strange formations which were fairly smooth on top, with stumpy rounded icicles beneath.

If you broke a bit off, it resembled a set of ice dentures. The sand was duned, with a light scattering of crunchy, sparkling snow.

I went into a local shop, but the shopkeeper refused to accept my 100 rouble note. On making enquiries, I discovered that old roubles were no longer valid – though one could change them in a bank until the end of the month. The government had knocked some noughts off: 1000 old roubles were now worth

10. As it was very near the end of the month, I had no time to spare.

Next morning, I queued in the bank in Lenin Street. When I reached the clerk, I was told they had no new roubles and I must go to the bank in Bankovskaya Ploshad. So I trudged over there, and joined another queue. Nothing much seemed to be happening, so I walked past the line into the main hall, where I was blocked by an armed policeman, who asked to see my blanka (form).

I asked him what form, and he pointed to a door in another building, where there was another long line.

When I at last reached the front, the policeman there asked to see my passport. "But", I protested, "I'm only exchanging old roubles for new ones."

He insisted that I needed a passport, so with silent curses I walked home.

I returned in a foul temper: this was one of my 'I hate Russia' mornings! After waiting in the queue, the young policeman on duty came out of his office, locked the door, and vanished. I groaned. It was probably his lunch hour. However, I was in luck: he reappeared quite soon and, as none of the other people queuing seemed inclined to move, I jumped the line and took a chair at his table. I tossed my passport at him and scowled. He examined it with evident interest, looked straight at me with a pair of beautiful grey eyes, favoured me with a delicious smile, and wanted to know why I was there. He then filled in my form for me, took me by the elbow, locked his office up again, and personally escorted me back inside the main bank, where I jumped yet another queue. I suppose I ought to have felt a bit ashamed but, frankly, sometimes it is good to be a foreigner and to get preferential treatment.

I left the bank with my new roubles in a good mood and stepped out into the square, where I was very nearly knocked for six by a police car. I cursed the driver (police had a tendency to drive like maniacs) and dusted myself down. One policeman standing in a small group on the corner nearby leapt towards me, took my arm, yelled at the driver, and courteously manoeuvred me across the square to the further side. It was my Don Juan policeman!

On Friday, 27th March, NATO bombed Kosovo. Many Russians were angry and shocked. There were enormous demonstrations outside the American Embassy in Moscow: no bombs, but eggs and rotten tomatoes were thrown.

Several of my students were worried that this would lead to war.

I went round to my student Vladimir's flat the next day, to send an email, as my computer was playing up. Ever since the lesson when he had nearly biffed the aeronautics engineer in my mature beginners' class for rubbishing Sholokov, we had formed a close friendship. He had kindly offered to let me send emails home. I met his wife, an electrical engineer who came from a long Cossack lineage, and they invited me to stay for tea. I asked them both what they thought of the Kosovo affair. Vladimir agreed with me that it would not lead to a major war, but Luda sadly shook her head. She told me she had relatives who used to live in that area but were eventually forced to leave when their water supply was deliberately poisoned. What a terrible mess.

Early in April, NATO dropped several more bombs on Belgrade. A British submarine was sailing towards Yugoslavia, and Russian ships were converging from another direction. People were protesting in cities all over the world.

Many Russians were angry about the bombing, but I suspected that, before long, they would forget in the daily travails of living in a recession. However, there are always the frustrated men, with no jobs or prospects, to whom the involvement and activity of war might be attractive. And the sad fact is that countries in recession often pick up in wars.

Few people I knew were talking much about the war. It was as if they were hoping that the whole explosive situation would just evaporate.

Of course, since so many countries – including Russia – have vastly reduced their regular armies, wars have become something else: the business of highly trained specialists with extremely effective weapons. Someone told me that Russia had the design for a military aircraft that was far more sophisticated than Stealth. It had not yet been manufactured, but could go straight into production if needed. That is, if the funds were there.

At the end of March, Valya told me she had seen some of our textbooks (which were expensive) in Sergei's safe when she asked him to put some money there for safe keeping. She asked me if I had put them there, which I hadn't. She added that she had noticed that some books were missing from her cupboard. I suggested that perhaps he had borrowed them for his own study before he went on his trip to England in April. However, we both knew that he had not been paid for months and that it was possible he had been selling some of our books to raise money. He had been doing quite a lot of trade selling CDs: strangers constantly came to his office, presumably in answer to his ads in the local papers. A bit of trading on the side to make ends meet was common everywhere and, though Sergei was undoubtedly a man of integrity, he was, after all, only human, and had dreamed of visiting Man United and the Beatles Museum for years.

I imagined how difficult it must be for the day staff to see all the money in the office from the students' fees, and all those tempting, beautiful English books which were available to them.

I was contracted to receive 500 US dollars a month, plus my flat and airfare. Actually, as I was now paid at ten roubles to the dollar, and the rate at that time was about twenty-six to the dollar, I was really receiving about 230 US dollars – peanuts! But to most Russians that was a lot of money at that time, and it was more than sufficient to live on.

I suggested to Valya that if she let Sergei know that she knew books were missing, whatever he was doing would stop – if he was doing it. However, over the next few days she was rather surly and unforthcoming with

Sergei, who kept asking her what was wrong. She clearly hadn't said anything to him but was feeling resentful and suspicious. I asked Genio what his advice was. He recommended quietly retrieving the books in the safe and then putting the incident behind her. Life was too short for resentments. As the days passed, these uncomfortable feelings gradually weakened and faded.

Vova told me there had been no work in his office, where they distributed goods to the port, for the past three weeks. He had nothing to do and wasn't being paid. He suspected the business might fold. There was a Dutch boat that had been marooned in the port for over a week because the crew had no Russian visas and were therefore not permitted to crew their boat up the Don to Kazakhstan, where they were supposed to deliver their cargo. They could theoretically get the boat towed up the river– but they hadn't enough money for that.

Also, three Red Star Line ships had been stuck in the port for several months. The company had gone bankrupt some time back, but apparently the Red Star Line was really a cover for other owners, and no one could discover who these owners were.

The wretched crew were isolated in their ships, unpaid, as nobody was prepared to take responsibility for the ships or the crew. Vova told me that various local people were donating food to the poor sailors.

Tolik, who had been unemployed for about two years, was hoping to open his own food business by the beginning of June. He had at last got a loan – at 80% interest! – but he seemed to think he could manage.

Everybody seemed to have a minimum of two jobs just to survive. Since Valya had taken over the running of our evening school, as well as teaching at the pedagogical college during the day, Genio had taken on most of the financial aspects in addition to his very responsible managerial job. I had nothing but admiration for the determination and ingenuity of these people.

On the 7th April, when I arrived at school, it was buzzing with all the day teachers. As they all looked cheerful, I surmised that they must have been paid. A few enquiries proved me right: they had just received their salaries for December!

People have asked me how on earth Russians could survive when they were not paid for months and there was no social security system. Well, it's amazing, but most of them did. Those with a little more helped those with less; since the very serious crash a few years ago, any money they had was stashed away somewhere safe rather than kept in banks. (See Chapter 25 for more information on the cost of living.) Most families had a cellar, loft or underfloor space absolutely stuffed with preserves which could feed them for months, and there was always barter.

Added to this, centuries of uncaring governments had ensured that people learned to look after themselves and their communities rather than assuming that they had a right to care from the State. They had little or no respect for the ruling elites and became experts at mending their own equipment, building their own homes, growing their own food, and avoiding taxes and other State demands as far as they could.

I remember being fascinated to watch the complete demolition of a big five-storey block of flats just by the tram track that I travelled on every day to school.

The block had stood empty all winter because it was considered unsafe and it was a real eyesore. Two weeks after the thaw, when the groundwater had bubbled underground, the deserted building was suddenly crawling with people, like an ants' nest. Bent old babushkas, lean old men with drinkers' noses, strong young men, girls and boys and women arrived with hammers, bits of scrap metal, levers, lengths of wood or just their bare hands, and pulled the entire building to the ground in just over a week. They carried their cargo off in old prams, homemade go-carts, shopping trolleys, on bikes.

After that, for about a mile in both directions, I could see neat piles of stacked bricks, wood, roof tiles and all the paraphernalia that, in combination, create a building, outside every home. Most building materials were owned by the State and it was difficult for ordinary people to get what they needed to repair their homes.

When my phone packed up, a delightful telephone engineer turned up to mend it. He was a hulk of a man, with a tiny bag which appeared to contain nothing more than a few bits of wire and one small screwdriver! He kept asking me whether I had this tool or that to which my reply was always, Sorry, no. In true Russian style, he was not the least bit thrown and improvised splendidly. For instance, he took a box of my matches and used several lighted matches to melt the plastic round a screw.

He was much amused by my phone system, which I tried to explain to him. The original phone was always substandard and had very poor reception. I could phone other cities in Russia, though after a call to Moscow or St Petersburg the phone often went dead for an hour or so, as if the effort had worn it out. I couldn't dial other countries, though my family could call me. Eventually, sometime before Christmas, the ring packed up. Tolik offered to fix it for me.

He arrived with one of his spare phones (he has several) and, by dint of twisting a whole lot of wires together in what appeared to me to be a hopeless knot, got the system working. The original phone sat on the floor and connected to the telephone exchange; the 'new' phone sat on the shelf, rang, and was used to speak into.

Perhaps, in the present climate in the UK, we, too, will become proficient at making and mending, instead of chucking appliances away and buying new ones.

25 THE COST OF LIVING

In 1991, at the time of the initial break-up of the USSR, the government decided, overnight, that 50 and 100 rouble notes were no longer legal tender. The idea behind this was to recirculate surplus cash that millions of Russians were hoarding in their homes, and to curb the black market. But the plan did not work. Black marketeers dealt mainly in US dollars or gold anyway, so their shady business was not affected. As usual, it was the ordinary citizens who suffered. By the end of that year, the average monthly wage was 400 roubles, and pensioners were lucky if they received 100 roubles. By early 1992, one month's average salary could be exchanged, at the official tourist rate, for 5 US dollars.

When I first went to Russia in November 1996, the exchange rate was 4.5 to 5 roubles to the dollar. Food prices remained pretty stable. The trams and public phones were free. Bus fares were about half a rouble.

By 1998, one could exchange a dollar for about 15 roubles. Monthly water rates were about 40 roubles, the monthly electricity bill was about 50 roubles (and rather higher if one had a gas cooker – work that one out!).

When I returned to Taganrog after a summer holiday in England in autumn 1998, the exchange rate was 27-30 roubles to the dollar. This rate fluctuated for a while and then settled down to about 27 roubles. Tram journeys now cost a rouble and one had to buy tokens for the public phones. The local mini-buses were 1.5 roubles. My flat cost 800 roubles p.m. – a fortune by Russian standards – and rose to 1000 in the final months of my stay.

In 2001, the average monthly salaries were as follows:

Primary school teacher	300-500 roubles
University teacher	500-800 roubles
University professor	1200 roubles max.
Small businessman	3000 roubles
Computer programmer	2000-2500 roubles

I'm no specialist when it comes to mathematics and economics, but it's clear that the average Russian had to struggle to make ends meet, and it is no surprise that they resorted to all sorts of activities to overcome this problem.

26 Music and Dance

I first came across 'The Taganrog Trio' in January 1997, when my student Igor invited me to the central Taganrog Museum with his son Artum. The museum was a handsome one-time palace and was fun. In one hall three musicians were rehearsing: a pianist, a violinist and a cellist.

On the rare occasions that I ate out in restaurants, for it did not seem to be something my friends did, there was always some live music – and the players of that music always seemed to be those same three musicians.

On a lovely June evening shortly before I returned to the UK, after my classes, a group of us decided to do a leisurely bar crawl, beginning in central Lenin Street, wandering through the park to the sea front, and then along to the port. My friend Tolik brought along a friend who he said had been wanting to meet me for some time. His friend Andrei arrived as we were sitting in a café where – surprise, surprise! – 'The Taganrog Trio' were hard at work. As we all left the café a few moments later, the trio were playing a very lively tune, and I couldn't resist dancing out. A moment later, my arm was hooked and I found myself lightly jigging out with Andrei. It was difficult to know how old he was, for he looked as if he was just out of school, and his friends called him Garc (short for garcon, as he resembled a smart waiter).

He was neat, small and fair-skinned with very dark curly hair, absolutely round black eyes and a soft, humorous mouth. He exuded enormous nervous energy and stammered slightly, as if he hadn't quite time to get all his words out. He comprehended English very well and insisted that I speak to him only in English, which he spoke hesitantly, yet eagerly. He had a raging curiosity about absolutely everything. I liked him enormously.

He was much amused when I hung back, on more than one occasion on our town trail, to set light to drifts of poplar seed. This annual event – known as the Pooch (the 'ch' pronounced as in loch) – is really rather remarkable, and much dreaded by all who suffer from lung weaknesses. The pavements and stairways seem to be covered in snow and the air is thick and ticklish.

If you put a lighted match to the fluffy seeds, they emit bursts and sparks of multi-coloured flame which shoots along the ground like a spluttering fuse. I could not resist that. By the end of that delightful evening, I felt that I had known Andrei for years.

One evening I was invited to an evening of Cossack song and dance. A student of mine, whose father used to be the Cossack chief for the entire region, told me he wasn't going to attend because his dad would be there. Surely, I remonstrated, you can cope with his company during a concert? He said most assuredly not: they would fight after ten minutes if they were anywhere near each other. He added that it was a tradition in his family that the men could not live in the same house. Clearly a case of the old bull and the young!

The entertainment was put on by the students of the teaching college. Both music and movement were extremely lively and most colourful and I thoroughly enjoyed the experience.

There was quite a gaggle of elderly Cossacks in the audience, wearing their red and blue uniforms, their chests drooping with medals, and I couldn't help wondering which of them was 'Dad'.

I also landed myself with a visit to a dancing school across town, courtesy of an FCE student called Viktoria.

I think she had overheard me asking some students if it would be possible to learn some traditional Russian dancing. What I actually experienced was the Russian version of 'Come Dancing'.

It took place in a rather splendid old hall – all blue and white, with enormous chandeliers and a parquet floor. Before the competition began, a pretty little girl with an enormous net bow in her hair solemnly sprinkled one handful (and she had small ones) of wood shavings over the floor. Then girls and matrons in gaudy frocks with loads of ribbons, bows, gauze, sparkles and feathers, faces heavily made-up, and elaborate hair-dos streaked in gold, silver, green and pink, grinned, pirouetted and curtsied to their partners before waltzing, polka-ing and tango-ing to a very cracked loudspeaker, playing music from the fifties and sixties as well as classical dance music. There were a number of minor collisions, as the hall was crowded, and one near-disaster when a dashing young man skidded and did the splits in very tight black trousers. It was fun, though not really my thing.

I finally made my excuses to Viktoria and politely declined her invitation to join the dancing school classes the following Sunday.

On a more serious note, I was very impressed that all young people in Taganrog were taught to dance. Whenever I found myself in a situation where dancing was on the cards – such as birthday parties, celebrations, wedding receptions – I had no problem in finding dancing partners who knew how to move to music and enjoyed doing so. A far cry from the UK.

27 THE ENGLISH CLUB

One of the advantages of living on my own my final year was that, first, my Russian greatly improved, and, secondly, I became much more sociable and adventurous and deepened my relationships with local people.

I didn't realise this, as Jonathan was a private, shy individual, but he had been running an English Club in the Taganrog Central Library. When he asked me whether I would be interested in taking over, as he felt he had enough on his plate, I agreed to give it a try.

The club was held on Wednesday mornings in a rather chaotic but comfortable sitting room in the library, and was open to anyone who wanted to improve their spoken English. Most of the regulars were undergraduates and graduates from the university and institutes, though others came and went. I enjoyed listening to their opinions and learned a good deal more about their culture.

Although a theme was always selected for the following week, as it gave the less confident speakers a chance to think about the subject and look up suitable vocabulary, conversation topics ranged wide. We talked about pantomime, the death of traditional theatre and music as a result of Communism, the fact that, until very recently, left-handed people were forced to use their right.

Other topics I recall were catacombs, the power of stones, cannibalism and other aberrant behaviour, insects and their amazing ability to survive – all subjects that one member or another threw up.

One regular, Andrei, suddenly disappeared for several weeks. He was a shy young man who sometimes gave the impression of not being quite all there, but would then surprise one with a most perceptive and original remark. He told us that he and some friends had travelled to ByeloRussia to sell food and buy products there to sell back in Taganrog. Products like rice were rationed there and could only be bought with coupons, so they had no difficulty selling all their food. They bought furniture to sell back home, but they were stopped and searched at the border and all the goods they had bought with their takings were confiscated as they were accused of being smugglers. He was obviously disappointed but just shrugged his loss off with a wry smile. I wonder who benefited from that furniture!

When the chosen topic was food – always a popular subject in Russia – I decided to bring in my large jar of marmite. Everybody tried some, and the majority thought it was absolutely disgusting. It is an interesting fact, though, that the odd Russian who liked the taste became positively addicted.

My students Tolik and Roman, for instance, liked it so much that I brought extra jars just for them. I also discovered in this session that most Russians dislike olives. They were all astonished that I don't like sturgeon or caviar – too oily and salty for me.

In one session the main topic of conversation was technology and labour-saving devices. We talked about computer viruses and got onto the subject of the psychology of perpetrators, which was interesting.

On the numerous devices and gadgets that are now available, we were generally agreed that there were fors and againsts. They can create more work rather than saving time.

I told everyone that, in England, I had several devices that were rather old or second-hand and, as I was inept when it came to technology, I was often driven up the wall when they went wrong – which they quite often did. Whilst here, in Russia, I had nothing more complex than an electric kettle and toaster, and housework was a gloriously simple affair. Once a week I shoved all my laundry in the bath with some soap, stamped on it with bare feet, left it to soak, and then hung it on the lines outside.

I cleaned the flat with a cloth and a twig broom, and occasionally dragged the rugs outside for a thump or covered them with snow and left them for a few hours first. They were much amused.

When we once got onto the subject of neighbours, an English teacher from the Institute called Irina told us she was wedged between one family who played hard rock day and night, and another who played the worst kind of Russian Pop at full blast, while she played Bach and Beethoven on the piano. Unlike most people, she looked forward to electricity cuts (quite common) because she could then take her revenge. She was very knowledgeable about Russian culture and European art and music.

Another week, Irina arrived bursting with enthusiasm about one of the articles in my Weekly Guardian, which I passed on to those that wanted. It was about an exhibition at the Barbican of Russian paintings from just before the revolution. She also enthused on an obituary to Dirk Bogarde, whom she said she greatly admired as an actor. When I asked her which of his films she had seen, she admitted she had only watched The Doorkeeper as none of his other films had been shown. It made me realise how culturally cut off many people here were. Her subject was cultural studies and she took great pains to keep up with events as far as she was able.

Another student, Tanya, mourned the fact that there was so little material for her final thesis on teaching methodology – everything was so out of date. Given these facts, it was no surprise that most Russians I knew were passionate about the Internet.

I discovered that they all loved Scottish kilts, and everyone wanted to know what – if anything – they wore underneath. I admitted that I hadn't looked, but I was sure they wore pants as Scottish dancing could be every bit as energetic as some Russian traditional dances and the kilts were liable to fly into the air. I told them that the different patterns on the kilts represented the various clans or tribes, and that my family belonged to two clans, the Campbells and the Robsons. When I recounted the terrible massacre of Glencoe, when the Campbells murdered the McLeans by subterfuge, they were fascinated. I asked them what articles of clothing from the past they would like to bring back, and they decided that handpainted fans would be fun.

After my experience of a Russian 'sauna plus birch twigs' (see Chapter 29), I told the members of the club about it. They, in turn, described the old Russian stoves, which used to be traditional in all homes. Irina even drew me a picture. The craftsmen who made them were highly valued and respected in the community. They were huge – like small rooms within rooms.

There was a brick base, with a big metal door into which one stacked the fuel – coal or wood. On top was a metal sheet where one could boil water and cook. Above that was a large brick oven with another metal door, where you baked – and when I say 'you', I mean just that! As well as baking bread in there, people used to lay damp straw on the base, put containers of water inside, and then climb in, pull the door to, and steam and sweat. No doubt the Hansel and Gretel stories originate from this practice. All households possessed a long sort of fork, ending in a horseshoe shape, which fitted exactly round the neck of big stoneware or clay pots used to hold water and for cooking, so that they could be drawn out safely when hot. Above this oven was the bed – nice and cosy I would imagine. And finally, there was the round metal chimney, also containing several small doors to release steam and keep the whole house warm. The complete structure would have been the centrepiece of the home during the long winter months.

At the English Club, there was never any problem in getting people talking. They were all intensely curious about life outside Russia, and questions came thick and fast. I would like to have talked more about their culture, rather than gleaning facts indirectly, but I realised how important it was to the members to talk to a genuine Brit who had travelled a good deal. They were a good crowd and I enjoyed the experience a lot.

28 People, Parties and Public Holidays

I can roughly categorise my time in Taganrog into three distinct periods. My shortest stay, from November 1996 to June 1997, was a tough learning period: discovering how to teach and developing my own distinct style; learning the basics of the language; gradually familiarising myself with the locale. I didn't socialise a great deal, and spent much of my free time with Paul, Valya and Genio, and later Lena, Ina and Vova – all good English speakers – or on my own.

September 1997 to June 1998 was a year when I came up against many of the frustrations that regularly tried local people and consequently became tougher and more resourceful. The longest stint was from September 1998 to July 1999. This was when I lived alone, deepened my friendships and became more settled. I was much more sociable and took a more active part in the politics of the school. Friends often dropped by uninvited, I entertained more regularly and received hospitality from them.

I received a call from an English missionary from Leeds, Elder Sharp, who was a Mormon. He said he'd heard a lot about me – I don't know from what source. As it was Jonathan's birthday the following week, I decided to throw a small dinner party for him, and invited his landlord Andrei and Andrei's delightful little daughter Nika, together with Elder Sharp and his colleague, Elder Hunter.

Both missionaries were very young: I found it quite difficult to call them 'Elder'! Elder Sharp was somewhat opinionated, and made it clear that they were not encouraged to drink tea, coffee or alcohol and must eat only 'healthy' food after blessing it first. Elder Hunter – a small, pale, slim 30-year old from Salt Lake City was more engaging. He was very pleased to be offered a meal and I suspected was feeling a bit lost and homesick. I had cooked a mild chicken curry with lots of vegetables and wondered whether the two missionaries would eat it. Thankfully, they did.

The next day, Sunday, I bumped into Vova in the market, and he invited me back for brunch. Sonya – their crazy Afghan hound – was in deep disgrace.

She had rifled the fridge, and then tried to bury her porridge in Vova's jeans! Vova stalked about the flat like a beautiful panther. He was trying to give up smoking, at Ina's suggestion, and was just about ready to kill somebody.

In the evening, at the telegraph office, I bumped into my old landlord, Vitaly, who was in his usual corner. He told me he had been looking out for me and thought I may have returned to the UK. He looked so thin and lean under his layers of winter clothing and my heart went out to him. He was always interesting to talk to, and so gentle and courteous, and I genuinely missed his company.

A delightful student who joined one of my classes in my second year, but left as soon as she wised up to the fact that Anya was possibly 'cooking the books', was Galya. She was a most attractive Ukrainian in her thirties, a vivacious lawyer with a love of life.

As a young woman, she became seriously ill from the effects of the Chernobyl nuclear plant explosion, and her family persuaded her to move away, which is how she came to live in Taganrog. She was determined, however, to end up somewhere else, and managed to find time for computer dating in addition to all her other activities.

In early April Galya received several beautiful red roses from an Englishman she had been computer dating. I asked her whether she was planning to visit him, to which she replied: "No, but he might visit me this summer." "Great" I replied. "No," she said. "He vill not like Taganrog. I am ashamed." Valya then piped up that Russians were often embarrassed by the dirt, inefficiency and poor service when foreigners visited. It was true that to visit the town in summer could be difficult. The previous summer temperatures were in the forties for two months; many homes had practically no water for several weeks; and one is not advised to swim in the Azov Sea from July through to early September because a vigorous weed turns the water pea green. However, I defended their town: it had its own charm and they shouldn't be ashamed of it. What was more, their warmth, hospitality and humour made up for any shortcomings.

Two weeks later, Galya invited me to a double birthday party in her law firm. Their offices were in some rather handsome rooms above a hotel. The boardroom table was groaning with food and bottles of champagne, vodka and cognac.

It was 2.30, but as far as I could see no member of staff was on call to answer the phone! Birthdays are important in Russia, and work can wait. And why not?

After toasts to the two birthday girls, we all dug in. Then the head of the firm – a big, cuddly, talkative man– read a poem written by the staff to each woman, each poem having been elegantly printed on an enormous card. Apparently this was standard practice for any birthday in the firm.

More talk and eats, and then the three men disappeared. They returned a short while later, in costume. The boss was God, draped in a white sheet with a rather wobbly halo over his head. He was accompanied by a large, shy angel with teensy cardboard wings, a smaller halo and a laurel crown. Finally, there was the Devil, in suggestive black tights with a red, piggy nose and huge pink and green ears.

They mourned the way the world was going and decided they would have to try and improve things for the two lovely birthday girls. Before them was a table covered with a cloth, and from time to time they peered under the cloth and drew out various objects which they mulled over. It was very funny. I was sorry to have to tear myself away betimes, and arrived fifteen minutes late for my class.

On the Sunday it was Olya's birthday, so I called on her family, bearing a present. I was given a warm welcome by people and animals alike; they had three dogs, three cats and three kittens. The four-week old kittens were enchanting and seemed to have numerous other mothers. Roni, the six-year old terrier for whom I sometimes dog sat, still had milk from her pups, who had sadly died, and the kittens happily suckled her, after which she picked them up and groomed them. One-year old Vilma, the Alsatian, took their heads gently in her mouth and licked them energetically, and even 6-month old Alsatian Peri sometimes babysat. The real mother occasionally wandered in to feed her brood, leaving the rest of the work to the dogs.

We all sat down to red caviar, smoked cheese and other goodies, after which we took a leisurely walk in the park.

On the way home I bumped into Roman, who was learning all about iron and steel pipes for his new job as sales manager for the Metallurgical Plant. He was going to deal with India and was hoping to get a business trip there in due course. He was like a cork, that young man. Nothing could keep him down.

On Easter Sunday I was woken several times by the chiming of church bells. There were only three churches in Taganrog as most of them were razed to the ground after the Revolution. It is traditional for people to take painted hardboiled eggs or special Easter cakes shaped like round towers to the church to be blessed by the priest.

After Easter came the May holiday, which was celebrated on May 1st, after which many families took a two-week holiday. I wandered round to experience the May Day rally in October Square. There was a big crowd, plenty of old men sporting medals, a good band and lots of jolly hammer and sickle red flags and banners and huge pictures of Lenin. Later, Roman called in for a while with a bunch of fragrant lilac.

Then off to Ina and Vova's, with another bottle of champagne, some ham, and a large ripe pineapple that I happened to spot on a stall en route. A few other friends turned up and we all enjoyed a charcoal barbecue of sausages and spuds with fresh herbs and radishes. I walked home via the beach, passing clusters of family groups preparing their first shashliks of the year, for they all love barbecues. Sonya, the Afghan hound, followed me all the way home and stretched out comfortably on my divan like a rather moth-eaten Siberian rug.

May 4th was glorious, so I took a long run along the beach. There was a cool, playful onshore breeze and the silver sea was pitted with the dark silhouettes of at least two hundred little fishing boats, all facing south. Beyond them were two fairy tale yachts with delicately arched sails.

It was a day to gladden one's heart, so I decided to investigate the circus which had come to town. Most towns have a permanent site, and Taganrog's was beside the central market. It was a rather tatty area with a big, rusting frame over which the marquee had been erected. My ticket cost 25 roubles and was in the second row. I bought some popcorn to get in the mood.

I'm not a great fan of circuses in general, but I must admit I enjoyed this one immensely. There were three excellent male acrobats and a spectacular fire-eater, who also did all sorts of things on broken glass, deflected sharp knives off his stomach, and jumped through flaming hoops. There was one very good clown among the comic contingent, and the few animals looked extremely healthy and were cheerfully disobedient at times. There was a beautiful lioness cub of about nine months; two stunning pythons; three monkeys of different types; two pert white cockatoos, a handsome blue macaw and several green-ringed parakeets. Several children in the audience came in bearing branches of lilac and tulips, and ran up to various performers as they left the ring to present their gifts.

I hurried home to prepare a meal for Galya, who I had invited to supper when I discovered she had workmen in (to smarten her flat before her English beau arrived) and her living room was full of dust and chaos.

Everything was bubbling and ready to eat, but still no sign of Galya who was no great timekeeper. When the doorbell did ring, it wasn't Galya but my private student Luda, a tall, soft-spoken blonde divorcee who was hoping to get out of Russia and, of course, I invited her to join us.

When Galya arrived a few minutes later, she realised that she had a ladder in her tights and insisted on returning home to change them despite my protestations that it was only Luda and I and we didn't care a bit. Fortunately, the meal was of a kind that wouldn't spoil.

Since both Luda and Galya were computer-dating men from English-speaking countries there was plenty to talk about. It seemed to be quite the thing for Russian women to seek husbands abroad. Galya's internet contact, John, was due to arrive for a ten-day stay in a fortnight and she was understandably very nervous about it. I suggested she not try to make everything 'perfect' as this could create tension all round. Luda admitted she was trying to find a connection in Australia, but she was afraid she might be too independent for most men. I told her that had always been my trouble! It was a good girly evening.

29 Trips out of Town

Genio and Valya invited me to join them for a country outing. We drove to a village along the Miuse River as it widens towards the estuary and found a secluded little valley leading down to the water's edge. There were enormous numbers of snakes – water and land varieties – and Valya and I scared one water snake just before it snapped up a very large toad in the shallows. As we girls strolled along the sandy shore (Genio in true manly style was busy with a fire for the barbecue), we saw several recently shed snakeskins.

There were many butterflies, one of which was shaped like a fan with a wicked face on the lower part of its creamy wing so that it seemed to be always upside down. There were lots of shrieking gulls, a few great terns, and stately herons winging over the river, and swifts wheeling and plunging to catch mosquitoes.

Great thickets of perfumed wild lilac combined with the mouthwatering smell of shashlik browning over Genio's most proficient fire soothed head, stomach and soul.

It was a glorious day – the first really warm one - and we all visibly relaxed. Genio drove us back a leisurely roundabout way and I asked them both whether most of the villages were so strung out. They didn't appear to have any focal point. Genio replied that this was common in the region. Many villages were either alongside rivers or on dirt cliffs and ridges where they were less likely to be flooded, so they developed in a linear fashion.

Then, a few days later during the May holiday, I accompanied Vladimir and Luda on a trip to Novocherkassk, which was the centre of the Cossack community. The drive there took over two hours, on account of being stopped by traffic police for speeding! The cathedral had a splendid site at the apex of a hill and could be seen for miles around. It was rather dark and gloomy but had a nice feel to it – peaceful and cool, and it was pleasant to quietly sit and meditate there. It was clearly an important place for Luda, who burned a lot of candles and prayed before her favourite icons. I later suggested that it must have been difficult for orthodox Christians like herself during the years of Communism when churchgoing was frowned on. Her son Kostya gently corrected me. Apparently, during World War II the Orthodox Church did a great deal to support the Russian front, donating and collecting money, providing soup kitchens, and encouraging people to be patriotic and fight for the fatherland. As a result, churchgoing was tolerated, although, if one wanted to gain good posts in the party, being a known practising Christian was not helpful. We were all disappointed that the Cossack Museum was closed – and on a public holiday, too!

Two days later Taganrog was buzzing with news. Some said that Yeltsin had sacked Chernomyrdin and several other leading politicians; others that the politicians had resigned and there was a move to impeach Yeltsin. I popped round to Luda and Vladimir's flat after work to ask them about the situation. Luda believed that most of the government were corrupt and cared nothing for their country and its people – only for their own pockets.

Though she didn't support the Communists either, at least they were a known quantity. When I hazarded the opinion that maybe people were afraid for a change of government because they still remembered the hardships under Stalin – the purges and starvation – she agreed and added that most Russians were no longer interested in politics.

I also asked my FCE students what they thought of the situation. These were all people in their twenties and thirties. They mistrusted Chernomyrdin, because he agreed with everybody, and definitely wanted a younger and more forward looking government: but who?

They didn't want the Communists back because they feared that this would close Russia's doors to the outside world. When I heard their opinions I thought, by no means for the first time, how small the differences between countries and cultures really are.

The last weekend in May, Valya and Genio suggested I accompany them on a trip to visit their relatives. I was touched that they should ask me, and looked forward to the experience.

We set off early for Varonezh, where their elder daughter Maria was a student. Beyond Rostov we drove north, crossing the lovely River Donetsk, a tributary of the Don. We had a bit of a hold-up at Bogychar, where the bridge over the Don was being strengthened and was one-way English style stop-'n-start. While waiting in the queue of cars, I longed to take a dip in the river below.

I offered to drive for a while but Genio wouldn't let me, and he was certainly right. I hadn't brought my passport and didn't have a driving licence with me so, if anything had gone wrong, it could have been extremely awkward. He had a dinky little device that bleeped every time we approached a speed check, of which there were many. It was absolutely foolproof, for every time it bleeped, thirty seconds on there would be the police car. We reached the handsome town of Varonezh at about half-past three, where we called in briefly to see Maria, and left her younger sister Anna there for the night. We then drove on to the village where Genio's mother had a dacha.

The village was called Pervimaya (first of May) and was reached via a rutted, sandy track. We then jolted past an amazing 'New Russian' estate of enormous redbrick 'palaces' – each more outrageous than the last – which were surrounded, ironically, by dirt, dust and rubble. We passed by a large field and were then in the original old village. It was a bit like going through a mirror into an Alice-in-Wonderland scenario: clean, simple little cottages with heavy wooden shutters, surrounded by fruit trees and gardens stuffed with food. Nearly all the inhabitants were old and I wondered whether such villages would exist twenty years hence.

Genio's mother was a heavy, lined woman dressed like a peasant. She was evidently a tough, resourceful and intelligent individual and I took to her at once. Her summerhouse was quite primitive. Water ran through a pipe into a sort of cylinder with a little tap underneath to feed the sink. The toilet was an outdoor privy of the long-drop variety; the floors were bare; there was the minimum of furniture. But it was cosy and comfortable and the food was excellent and as fresh as can be.

The only dachas I had seen near Taganrog were actually much more basic, whereas this was a home from home where one could happily live throughout the spring and summer months.

The garden was a dream of fecundity, with about forty currant bushes, loads of fruit and nut trees, raspberries and strawberries with garlic planted along the rows to discourage pests. Dachas such as these were a lifeline to families in the past and still played an important part in many communities.

I much enjoyed my short stay in this village. The birdsong in the evening and early morning was glorious. I was not surprised to be given the 'masterbed' – in a niche behind a curtain – and very comfortable it was. I didn't know where the others slept – perhaps with a neighbour – and had learned not to ask as it would only offend.

The next morning we drove back to Varonezh to pick Anna up and then continued north-east for about two hours to the small town of Gryazi, where Valya's mother, Nina, lived. The houses were mostly wooden with pretty decorative window frames. Nina would be seventy-five the following day and the town was putting on a special do for her in the town hall as she was their local poet.

All Nina's family had congregated there for the occasion: her two brothers, Alexandr and Leonid; her two sons (Valya's half-brothers), Genio and Vladimir and family, and a charming cousin and his wife from Varonezh. Genio was a warm-hearted, politically active, barefoot priest in a long gown, who did carpentry in his spare time.

The house was largely furnished with his handiwork. Vladimir was a kind, toothy engineer, accompanied by his wife Tatiana and their daughter, who was mooning over a lad who looked about fifteen, but had just completed his military service, so must have been older. Nina herself was a small, round, gracious old lady with fine white hair coiled into a bun at the nape of her neck. She had a

TRADITIONAL SUMMER HOUSE

beautiful soft, rounded voice and a gentle slightly distrait manner. Actually, I discovered that she hadn't slept a wink the previous night for nerves. Like most Russian women I met, I suspected that she was tough and resilient.

Everyone bustled about, preparing an enormous feast in the tiny kitchen, and I felt rather redundant as nobody would let me do anything. So I went for a nosy walk.

We all dolled ourselves up and drove to the hall, which was packed. Nina obviously did a lot of work with the local schools because the first part of the entertainment was provided by groups of primary school children who danced, sang and recited some of Nina's poems. Nina herself then read some of her poems beautifully, after which a quartet of women singers sang several of Nina's poems, which had been transformed into songs by a man who arranged the musical backup.

Finally, all the members of the family, plus myself, were invited up onto the stage. I was very touched when Nina, making a short speech of thanks, mentioned 'the visitor from England', and I found myself stepping forward to give her a kiss and hug. We then drank champagne in a tiny back office before returning to the house for the feast. It was all very jolly and relaxed, and the men downed vast quantities of alcohol.

I was given the sofa bed in the living room, with a narrow passageway between my bed and the long dining table.

Valya and Genio were in the bedroom just off the living room. I have a hazy recollection of waking up in the night to see the milky figure of Valya, stark naked, leading her husband Genio by the hand past my couch, and whispering, "This way. No, here – mind the table, don't wake Gilli!" He presumably needed the privy and couldn't find his way. A short while later, Valya tiptoed back leading – I think, or did I dream it? – a totally different man!

I suspect several of the male contingent were blearily blundering about in the dark with overfilled bladders and Valya was taking them in hand! Generally speaking, Russian men were heavy drinkers whilst their women were not.

Being both a stranger, and foreign, this visit could have been rather an ordeal, and just at first it was. But one thing among others that living in Russia taught me was to graciously accept hospitality without feeling guilty or that one must always do something in return. It was an important lesson for me. The whole family treated me with great kindness and consideration and I felt privileged to share in that special celebration.

Driving from this small town, we had to pass through Lipitsk – a totally amazing place. It seemed to be one endless line of factories, a huge refrigeration plant and a vast metallurgical plant complex.

This last stretched for about 18 km, with tall columns of chimneys belching smoke, great cooling towers, enormous metal girders and great brick and concrete structures. The air reeked of coal and was very fumey. Genio indicated a fir wood and said that, some years ago, all the trees were brown and dead. They must have cleaned the place up a bit since then, as there was plenty of greenery. Genio sometimes visited this complex on business and told me that about 20,000 people worked there, though it used to be much more. When I exclaimed at the sheer size of this industrial site, he grinned and said I should go to Mariopol in the Ukraine, where there was an iron and steel plant four times as big.

It was a very hot day on that Sunday drive and I was full of admiration for Genio's driving skill and sheer tenacity. I estimated he must have driven over 2,000 km that weekend.

Three weeks before I left Taganrog, Galya told me we had been invited to have a Russian banya (steam bath) at the dacha of some friends of hers. I had quite often had saunas and ice-cold dips in England, but had never experienced the genuine Russian version and I was all for the experience.

I walked over to Galya's flat a little after nine, lugging three bags full of fruit, salads and boiled new potatoes as my contribution. Our taxi driver was a stunningly beautiful girl with short blonde hair and golden eyes who looked about twenty-three. She was chatty and we soon discovered that Natasha was actually forty, had a family of four and had had the job for two months and loved it. I asked her whether she had had any trouble with drunks. She grinned and said she was a judo practitioner and had no qualms about chucking a drunk out of the car if he got troublesome. There were apparently only three women taxi drivers, as most would be too frightened to do the job. We picked up a pretty girl, Oksana, who was the younger daughter of our host and hostess, and then drove along a potholed dusty track to the village of Bessergenovka (translated as 'without Sergei'). I wondered who Sergei was and where he went!

Our hosts were about my age – brown, plump and welcoming. Nina had a winning smile and gave the impression of never getting phased. Sasha seemed more hot-blooded and very energetic. Their dacha, which they had acquired ten years before and built by stages, was delightful. There was a cool, pleasant living room, with the minimum of furniture and no fuss and – God be praised! – a most welcome fan on the ceiling (temp. about 35oC). Three wooden, slatted chairs, low to the floor with angled seats and slightly reclining backs, particularly impressed me as they were so well-designed for backs which, alas, many chairs are not. I remarked on them and Sasha said he had made them himself to his own design and that the slatted sections were made from some apple boxes he had found.

The garden was full of fruit trees, vegetables and a variety of herbs, and Sasha had built a metal shower house, like a small tower, at one end – though he said there wasn't enough water to use it at this time.

After being shown round, Galya, Oksana and I wandered down to the sea, which was a 10-minute walk away. There was a lovely view across to the Taganrog peninsula and headland, with all the port cranes. Nearer to hand were wild flowers in profusion, basking lizards, humming crickets, and in and around the reed beds croaking frogs and chirruping birds. We also spotted a cuckoo. The sea was shallow and rather scummy and we saw a couple of sea snakes so we decided not to swim. Also, Galya told me that the previous week a ship carrying chemicals had an accident in the port and no one knew how much of the chemical effluent had seeped into the sea.

We returned to the dacha for a light lunch of various salads and a delicious homebrewed alcoholic drink made from raspberries. Sasha told me he was a builder and had worked in Nigeria for three years constructing a big metallurgical plant. It was an international operation, including French, Spanish, German and Russian workers. I asked him whether the money was good. He laughed. The other nationalities were paid US$3000 per month; the Russians received US$300.

Galya reminisced about her childhood in a small town in the Carpathian Mountains in the western Ukraine. Her maternal grandparents had a dacha in the hills. One day, as a little girl, she accompanied her grandmother to the spring to fetch water and pick blackberries. When Galya spotted a dog and two puppies by the stream, she ran over to them and started stroking the pups. Suddenly, she heard her grandmother calling her urgently and ran up the slope to join her. Her granny, much perturbed, told her the dogs were in fact wolves.

She also related an interesting incident about a bear. She and her family used to ski in the mountains. At the pension where they stayed, guests were always warned to take sugar lumps in their pockets in case they met the resident bear, which was prone to demand sugar from skiers.

One woman didn't believe this and went off to ski on her own one morning. A big bear lumbered up to her and stretched out its paw. She had no sugar to give it. It then patted her pocket to make its request clear – and broke her hip. As a last resort, it patted her shoulder, as if to say 'Oh well, dear, never mind!', and broke that too. Some other skiers later found her and carried her down the mountain to safety.

After our leisurely lunch, we all walked through the growing heat to a very pleasant little stream. The water was very clear and cold and tumbled from a small waterfall between steep wooded banks. We all took brief glacial dips and then clambered about the banks.

By the time we got back, the bathhouse was ready. It had a raised wooden shelf for lying/sitting on, the heater in one corner, and a big churn full of cold water with a scoop. Galya and I went in first. It was the hottest sauna I have ever had! Nina had marinated various herbs in a bucket and we poured this pungent water over the boards, poured some water on the bricks, and then gasped and sweated. Galya had brought a jar of honey mixed with salt which we massaged over each other. After a while, Nina came in and thrashed us with damp birch twigs – a common part of a Russian sauna! – which hurt quite a bit. After another sweat, we got dressed and sank into Sasha's comfortable chairs in the living room. In came the barbecued meat, salads, fruit, some homemade samogon (alcohol) and lemon tea. Then back into the bathhouse for another sweat.

Finally, there was sleepy talk on the porch until Natasha returned to drive us home. What a peach of a day that was!

30 Water, Water Everywhere, and Not a Drop to Wash in

For my first two stints in Taganrog, I returned to England in early June, so I had not experienced the full heat of summer. That was to come in 1999.

Things began to heat up towards the end of May. And as the heat increased, the supply of water decreased. I recall returning to my flat on a hot, muggy night after classes, to find not a drop of water issuing from the taps. I washed my feet in some yucky water left in the washing-up bowl, rinsed my mouth from a bottle of drinking water, and fell gratefully into bed.

The next day I christened 'the day of smells'. On first rising, my nostrils were assailed by a vile smell of drains. After bolstering myself with a cup of coffee, I checked the toilet and poured strong bleach down both the loo and bath outlet– something I would not normally do. The outlets for both the sink and basin were always so poor that I had used plastic bowls to pour used water down the bath or toilet, hence the problem.

On venturing out, I was struck by the heady scent of the acacias, which were in bloom. That was good. Then, in the evening, I was knocked for six by the stink of highly toxic paint from about thirty freshly painted desks and chairs in the school hall. As the day school had closed until September for the summer break, staff and parents were busy mending and decorating. By midway through our second lesson, I suggested a 10-minute pause outside as we were all feeling faint and nauseated. We later voted on whether it would be preferable to die of asphyxiation or cold (there was a chilly wind that night) and we all voted to throw all windows open.

By the end of the first week in June the temperature was constantly in the lower 30s and the pooch (the fall of cotton-woolly poplar seeds) was horrendous: the downy seeds floated up nostrils, into eyes, ears and mouth; strayed into one's food and heaped into unsweepable carpets on floors and pavements.

In the Communist era most schoolchildren were sent to socialist holiday camps for several weeks, but now they were too expensive for most families, and so the beaches were crowded with noisy children and teenagers practising judo and taking leggy runs. In no time, the sand was littered with Russian detritus of all kinds, including broken glass, and my barefoot runs came to a halt.

I yearned for some peaceful corner somewhere, and was graced with an offer from Luda and Vladimir to use their bathroom should I need it, as their water supply was okay. Visiting them was like finding a cool, peaceful oasis out of a sandstorm: quiet voices; soft ripples of laughter; a clean cloth spread on the table with excellent Earl Grey tea and one of Luda's delicious cakes; and, of course, clean water. What angels they were. When I bussed over to Olya's home for her private lesson I found everything in confusion, which was unlike the family. Mother Olga was exhausted and admitted to me that she was finding her job of writing Russian language books for primary school children more and more demanding.

Vassily looked pale and drawn and disappeared into his study to lie down. Olya could not concentrate at all, so I cut the lesson short and advised her to rest as much as she could and to reduce the hours of revision before her FCE exams, as her English was excellent.

On a slightly cooler day (my thermometer read 26oC), I met Vladimir and Luda's son Kostya, staggering with two buckets of fresh water from the local pump. They also now had no water! How could there be serious water shortages when we were surrounded by rivers and sea?

WATER. It was the main topic of conversation everywhere.

The previous year, there were serious summer water shortages in the town centre but not in the suburbs. This year, all homes seemed to be affected. To make matters worse, the times when the water was turned on were unpredictable.

One would leave the bath taps on, the plug in, and buckets under each tap in hopes of catching any water that issued forth.

My ears became so attuned to the wonderful sound of plashing water that, if I was asleep, I would wake on the instant, leap to the bathroom, throw off clothes and have a shower and hairwash, throw dirty clothes into soapy water….

Galya told me that the town council had decided to improve the town's ancient water system and appealed to a specialist German company to give them help and advice. The Germans said that the first thing was to take samples of tap water from all over the town, which was done. The results of the analyses were rather shocking. Not only should nobody drink the water, which of course many Russians did because they couldn't afford to pay 16 roubles for a 5-litre bottle of drinking water, but no one should wash in it either. When the first gush of water came out of a tap, it was often yellowy-brown and smelled of rust and decay. It was good news, though, that the council were taking the problem seriously, and were planning to gradually replace the old pipes.

By the last ten days of June, the temperature was in the forties. Friends told me that the long-range forecast for August was twenty degrees hotter!

When Roman phoned to suggest I joined him and Tolik for some windsurfing that sounded like a good idea. I met up with Tolik – pink, sweaty and jaded from work - and we took a tram to the boatyard. The surfer belonged to Roman, and was big and heavy. I managed eventually to raise the sail, but got no further than that. I could see Tolik was dying to have a go so I handed it over to him. The beach was packed with people and dogs, and the sea lukewarm, greenish and slightly soupy, but there was a heavenly breeze and a soft, lilac sunset. We didn't leave the beach until about ten and all felt much better for the cool.

There were a couple of days near the end of June when it was a bit cooler. After classes and a quick, light supper, I strolled down to the beach for a swim. There was a two-thirds very bright moon. The tide was right down, leaving plenty of large shallow pools glowing in the moonlight. I was enchanted to find masses of sand drawings and sculptures, the best of which was a naked woman who seemed to be just forming out of the sand, like the birth of Venus. There must have been a competition earlier.

I didn't in fact swim. The sea was too shallow. But I paddled dreamily. The flat, soft ripples winked and beamed and – as I gazed out to sea – I got the impression that the whole world was in motion, which of course it is. I had never lived by a large expanse of water before and it was something I would miss. The Azov coast is not especially pretty or dramatic but I had learned to love it in all its manifestations. And I somehow knew, in my heart, that I would not be returning the following year.

31 THE FRIDGE SAGA

Valya had been asking me whether I would return to the school the following year. In many ways I wanted to continue, but my intuition kept troubling me. Eventually, I decided to follow my inner voice, because that had proved to be more reliable in my life than my tendency to charge into things with the minimum of planning. As it turned out later, my intuition was right. I was needed back in the UK. The word got around in no time and it may be that my landlords also got wind of this.

For whatever reason, Zoya started popping in unexpectedly and shuffling around. She seemed to have a fixation about the fridge! Every time she turned up, she would open the fridge door and then ask me when I last defrosted it. I assured her I defrosted it regularly (which I did) and tried to be welcoming. She also began muttering about illness and poverty and eventually it became clear to me that she was trying to either get me out or get an agreement to raise the rent.

As the rent was paid by the company, I passed this on to Valya who raised her hands in horror. The rent was already extortionately high for Taganrog and there was no way she was going to pay more.

A few days later, I went into the school office during the break and Valya waved her arms extravagantly and mimed that I should be silent. She was on the phone. She then passed the receiver over to Sergei who made the most extraordinary whistling sounds, tapped the side of the receiver, and replaced it in its nest.

"Who was that?" I asked. "Your bloody landlady," she replied. "She wants more money and I won't pay her another rouble." The phone rang again. Sergei picked it up. "Magazin (shop)" he said briskly. This happened another three times before Zoya gave up. Predictably, she turned up at the flat the next morning. She wanted me to phone Valya. I told her that I'd mislaid my phone book. She then once again regaled me with a sob story so I adopted the Russian style. I made her a cup of tea, sat her down, and then told her I knew perfectly well the rent was already outrageous and that she would not get another rouble. She then said she needed me out of the flat by 26th June It was then the twelfth and I reminded her that we had agreed I would stay until early July. .

I found my diary and pointed to the page for 4th July. "That's when I leave," I said. "You can move new tenants in after that." She seemed to take the point.

On the fifteenth, I was just about to sit down to lunch, when Zoya's husband let himself in. He hobbled about from room to room with his stick thumping and his lame leg dragging, muttering and tsk-tsking about the state of the flat. He then had the gall to ask me when I last cleaned it.

It was in a perfectly respectable state apart from a bit of sand on the floor, which would be swept up at the weekend. He then poked into the fridge and told me I needed to defrost it, which I'd done a fortnight before. Finally, he told me he wanted me out by 24th June. His manner was altogether aggressive and unpleasant. I'd had quite enough of him by this time so I opened the front door and asked him to leave. I pointed out that the rent had been paid to the end of June and, until then, the flat was mine and he had no right to come barging in. Hanging onto the door with one hand, he flourished his stick like a Kalashnikov – pointing it directly at my heart – and yelled that he had fought in the Great Patriotic War. I didn't think it was worth riposting that the war ended more than half a century ago and that any Russian man with two legs would have been a soldier then. I waited until he ran out of breath and then waved my hand towards the stairs and barked "Leave!" And he did.

Five minutes after he left, Zoya phoned to ask if he was there. I told her he'd just gone and slammed the phone down. She kept on trying to phone me so eventually I left the phone off the hook. Poor Valya and Sergei. What a pair!

I seriously considered asking Galya, who had a little spare room, whether I could camp with her for the final ten days and suggested this to Valya next day. She thumped the desk and declared "Absolutely not!" She couldn't bear the couple: they deeply offended her sense of what was Right and Russian. From a few chance remarks, I learned that my neighbours in the block didn't think much of them either.

On the Friday of that week I was surprised to see Valya in the office. She had told me that she had to invigilate exams and interviews for potential applicants to the pedagogical institute. "What are you doing here?" I cried. "I've come to pay you," she replied. "Oh Valya! You could have waited till Monday! We won't starve!"

I hugged her. She was looking exhausted. She then asked me what my plans were. "About what? I never have any plans!" "Did you defrost your fridge?" What was it with Russians and fridges? "As a matter of fact, I defrosted it last night. And cleaned all the windows to boot!" "Oh, thank God!" "Why?" "Because that damn Zoya woman phoned me again today. She said if Gilli hadn't defrosted her fridge she would send in the police. So I cried, 'Okay. Go ahead and call the police, and I'll call in the tax inspectors.'" She knew perfectly well that they would not have declared that they were letting the flat. We laughed all the way to the tram stop.

On the 23rd June I was still unsure whether I'd have to move out the next day. Valya had ordered me to stay put – she was determined to fight this one out – but what if Alexandr turned up at crack of dawn with workmen and new tenants? I wouldn't put it past him. I had asked Galya if I could stay with her, if necessary, and she had assured me that would be fine.

I decided to play safe, so I stayed in and spent the best part of the day beating rugs out in the yard, cleaning all the floors and walls, the cooker, the fridge, and dispensing with the remaining rubbish. Fortunately, there was water for twenty minutes early that morning, so I had lots of bowls, bottles and buckets full of it. However, I decided not to pack. If

Alexandr did materialise, he would have to wait a couple of hours.

When I approached my block after work I spotted Alexandr lurking but he hadn't seen me. I scuttled round the corner to calm myself, then entered the block and climbed the stairs to my flat. The door wouldn't open, and for a moment I thought he must have replaced the lock, but then I heard faint sounds from the other side of the door.

I rang the bell. Alexandr opened the door, pointed at me theatrically with his index finger, and barked, "Leave!" I was momentarily taken aback, but then realised he was mimicking my previous behaviour. Touché, Alexandr! I laughed, and meekly admitted I couldn't leave yet as all my possessions were inside. He let me in.

Zoya was in there, scrubbing the bath and using up all my precious water. I gave Alexandr a letter that Valya had written to him. He read it without comment and then asked me when I was going to leave. I repeated that it was the fourth of July. It seemed, then, that they were going to let me stay: no tax inspectors for them! We were all perfectly civil to one another, in true Russian fashion. However, that was not the end of it. Three days later, Alexandr turned up again in the afternoon. He did his usual thumping around with his stick and I chose to ignore him and carried on reading. So he came right up to me and demanded to know when I had last cleaned the bath. I ignored that, too. After half an hour of silent warfare – with him stomping about and me attempting to read – I decided to leave early for school, packed my rucksack and walked out to the hall.

Alexandr was standing there, naked except for his underpants! I stalked past him and locked the door behind me. I suspected he was more than a little mad.

On my return, I found that half the furniture had been moved – quite unnecessarily. My sponge had clearly been used to clean the bath or something, and stank of some awful cleaning fluid. It also looked as though my flannels had been tampered with.

I threw them all out. Some of Alexandr's clothes were hanging on hooks in the bathroom. Also, I noticed some blood on the hall floor. What had the man been up to? Mainly, he infuriated me, but there was a sense in which he scared me. He seemed capable of anything. I took a deep breath. I only had three more days to tolerate his behaviour and there was no way I was going to surrender now. Like Valya, my battle lines were drawn up.

On July 1st, when I was taking an afternoon nap as it was extremely hot and thundery, I was woken by the constant ringing of the bell. It was Alexandr. He spent the entire afternoon doing things in the bathroom and toilet and creating an enormous amount of mess and noise, but I was too tired and hot to protest or go out. Valya turned up in the evening, and was tearful about my leaving, and I felt close to tears myself. She overcame her misery by having a jolly good row with Alexandr! When Zoya also appeared, I decided to appeal to her. She was a woman, after all, and wasn't half as bad as her husband. Indeed, had she not been married to such a monster I think she would have been okay!

I pointed out that if her husband continued to do DIY jobs in the flat while I was still there I would be unable to give the place a final clean after I had packed.

If she could persuade him to leave me be for the next two days I promised that they would not regret it.

I always left rented accommodation in good order. She took the point and spoke to him. His response was: "Why shouldn't I come? I won't bother her."

My heart sank somewhat, but I noted an obstinate fix to Zoya's jaw and hoped that she would bring her recalcitrant husband round later. She must have prevailed, for Alexandr did not invade my space again until the day of departure.

32 I HATE TO SAY "GOODBYE"

I've always hated saying goodbye, perhaps because I have moved so many times. For many years I protected myself by practising my leave-taking in advance and then sort of switching off, which must have been hurtful to people who cared for me. That is, until I discovered that creating some kind of farewell ritual eased the discomfort for all. So I decided I would organise a special event for any friends who could come. The first thought was to hire a yacht and crew for the day, but friends gasped in horror and explained that it was far too hot, and the sea too green and gungy, and nobody would enjoy it. Then Vladimir, who was always full of practical ideas, suggested that I hire a holiday camp venue for a weekend.

He also offered to set it up for me if I let him know how many people were coming. What an angel! I spent the next few evenings after school ringing round. Quite a lot of people could not make it for one reason or another, saddest of which – for me – was that Vova would be away on business for ten days. I called round to see him and Ina the day before he left. We had a simple supper in their little garden, where we were bitten nearly to death by mosquitoes, and when I kissed Vova goodbye I wondered whether I would ever see this very dear friend again. They told me they were hoping to have a child before long, and would I be godmother. I joyfully assented and blinked rather too much to hold back tears.

On the morning of departure to the holiday camp, I rose bright and early to do a vast food shop. I'd arranged for all friends who were without their own transport to convene at a point in the centre of town, where a bus would pick us up. The bus, which was ancient, dusty and obviously used for camping as it had sort of bunk beds rather than seats, arrived on time, and we all piled in. We were Vladimir, Luda, their young nephew and niece, Ina, Galya and little Olya. Genio, Valya and family were arriving separately in their own car, as was Kostya.

The camp was near the Miuse estuary on the River Leman. Though the buildings were somewhat cracked and crumbly, they were softened and enlivened by lovely trees, including an avenue of limes in flower, and by the wide Leman with a little beach, earth cliffs and swaying reed beds. The large central building was closed, and we were consigned to a couple of mobile homes on stilts, each containing two rooms with four beds, a little living room and a small balcony. Bed linen was provided as part of the package, a fridge, and a long metal barbecue with a horseshoe metal prop for balancing pots. There was no cooker or washing facilities, but there was a loo. In other words, it was pretty primitive!

During the Communist period, when nearly all Russian children attended such camps for several weeks every summer at very little cost, this would have been a thriving summer community, with a central canteen, showers and toilets in plenty, and all sorts of entertainments. But times were now hard and the camp had decayed as a result.

Fortunately, Vladimir's family were hardened campers and mountain climbers, and they had brought everything but the kitchen sink in their car, which I discovered when Kostya arrived.

In no time, everyone was cheerful and busy, and clearly determined to enjoy themselves. We sorted out bedrooms, unloaded crockery, water bottles and bags of food, and began chopping up vegetables and preparing for the evening feast. The evening was sultry, so we then all sped down to the cool water for a glorious bathe.

We had moved three tables and most of the chairs outside under the trees. The sky was dramatic and wild. We all sat round the tables and dug hungrily into all the bowls of salad when the heavens opened. Kostya and Vladimir leapt up from their seats, sped to their car, and returned with a huge plastic sheet, which they hauled over the tables, chairs and ourselves. Our close proximity, necessitated by the size of our improvised shelter and the fact that we were its props, made for an affectionate and hilarious evening!

The storm had cleared the air and Sunday was wonderful. Everyone did their own thing and there was a very relaxed atmosphere. The teenage contingent buried Kostya – all six foot plus of him, bar his head – in the sand. I then lay on top of the mound, and they buried me too! The weight and cool of the sand was heavenly. I was so happy to see all these hardworking people, who rarely had time off, relaxing and enjoying themselves.

Throughout the weekend, there was a constant refrain of "Gilli! No!" – always from one of the men – whenever I started to lift anything or move some furniture. Clearly such activities were men's work – as was collecting and chopping wood for the barbecue, lighting and feeding the fire and collecting water.

Young Artum, Luda and Vladimir's nephew, took on the job of chopping kindling and logs with an amazingly sharp axe. I watched him with pleasure, for he was adept at the job, though only ten.

Half an hour before the bus was due, I suggested to Vladimir that we found a quiet corner to settle up. He said that wasn't necessary and that I should talk to Valya about it the next day. I felt immediately suspicious. I knew these people and I suspected he and Valya were up to something.

Genio and family left in their car, after hugs all round, Vladimir and Luda drove away, and the rest of us piled into the rattletrap bus. Arriving in Taganrog, everyone went their ways, though Kostya insisted on carrying my stuff and walking me home. Surprise, surprise! My front door would not open. I knew at once that my landlords were within. Sure enough, Zoya was footling about in the flat, and a young lad was fixing meshes to the windows. I tested the taps and, wonder of wonders, cool water literally gushed out. I left them to it and had a much needed hair wash and shower. Thankfully, they both left whilst I was still plashing and singing lustily in the bathroom. The next day, I accosted Valya in the school office and asked her how much I owed for the weekend. She gave me a rather garbled response, but as far as I could make out, she was suggesting that the school paid for the weekend. I replied very firmly that this was an outrageous suggestion: the school could not afford such luxuries; perhaps she should consider paying herself more salary; and, thank you very much, but this was my treat and I would pay for the hire of the bus and the camp. She laughed ruefully, looked mildly embarrassed, and agreed that I could settle up with Vladimir I placed the money in an envelope with an English postcard, on which I wrote that he was an excellent organiser and a stalwart friend.

The last week of June was both exhilarating and exhausting. Once the word got around that I was leaving, and would not be returning in the autumn, my doorbell was constantly ringing as students and friends called round to say goodbye, or to invite me round for a final meal. I had collected all the books, cds, essential oils and other paraphernalia that I had accumulated over three years and laid them out on the central table so visitors could select what they wanted. It was a relief to see the pile gradually diminish.

I suggested to Valya that she take most of the kitchen equipment, towels and so forth for the next teacher, and she accepted with alacrity, though I suspect Genio may have groaned. Where to stash it all?

Roman was so busy with work that he had not been able to join us for the weekend, but he popped round from time to time, always cheerful and energetic. One time it was to tell me that he had just received his FCE certificate. He beamed at me like a Cheshire cat, gave me a resounding kiss, and twinkled off. On another occasion, he turned up rather late one night to copy some music tapes, and to inform me that he would be going to Shanghai early in July with his boss, for some oil conference where they might sell their pipes. He asked me about suitable things to buy whilst he was in China (all Russians tend to do a bit of trade on the side in this way). I suggested silks and cottons as it was rare to find natural fabrics in Taganrog; perhaps also Chinese lanterns as they're light and foldable; and maybe jars and tins of interesting food. I offered him some of my books, which he accepted with alacrity and, before he left, he told me a Russian joke about the hammer and sickle flag. The Russian word for hammer can also mean 'to send your work to the devil' (or not to do it); the Russian word for sickle also has the meaning 'to avoid', especially with reference to national service. Thus the Communist flag actually represents idleness and avoidance of duty to the fatherland!

Tolik was another regular visitor during my final days in Taganrog. He was such a kind man, but seemed to invite bad luck. He was frequently short of money and his business ventures were extremely risky. One Sunday he arrived just as I was about to go to the market as I had practically nothing in the fridge. He offered to come with me, and persuaded me to buy a whole pike.

It was huge and expensive but I was too hot and floppy to argue. On account of its size, I then felt compelled to give a supper party so the gross thing could be eaten. We went to Tolik's flat and he prepared it for me. First, he laid sheets of newspaper in the bath and then skillfully scraped off all the large, armour-like scales. Then he used a hatchet to chop off all the spiny fins and the tail. He finally slit its belly, scooped out all its entrails and gills, chopped off its poor head, and axed it into thin chops ready for frying. After watching this procedure, with mixed feelings of admiration, curiosity and disgust, I took a taxi home and collapsed in a dizzy heap, before rousing myself to ring round and invite friends to partake of the chops.

Diana, a tall beautiful black-haired student from the pedagogical institute, told me it was her last lesson with me as she was off to Sochi to take her FCE exam.

I gave her my copy of Laurie Lee's Cider with Rosie together with a big hug. She joined my third class on my very first day – three years ago – and hadn't missed one class since then. She was calm, focused, and had great integrity. It would not surprise me if she ended up running her own school somewhere – perhaps in Dagestan, where her grandparents lived.

I also bumped into an ex-student, Volodya, who had been in the same class as Diana and had also attended from the first lesson. We were both in a post office queue. I was somewhat surprised to see him as he and his wife had applied for green cards to start a new life in Canada with their daughter and I thought all had gone according to plan. Indeed, I had even sent him a postcard from England the previous summer to wish the family well in their new life.

I tapped him on the shoulder and greeted him warmly, but he seemed strangely distant and almost unfriendly. Not like him at all. We spoke for only a moment, and I jotted my phone number on a scrap of paper and gave it to him.

I felt puzzled and a little hurt at first. On reflection, though, I suspected that – as a result of the economic downturn – the money he and his wife had been saving had lost its value. I knew that immigrants to Canada had to possess a minimum amount in order to qualify for admission.

Having probably received my postcard, he would have felt embarrassed and humiliated. How very sad.

I visited Olya's family to say goodbye. The flat was peaceful for once – none of the usual constant phone calls and comings and goings. Vassily, who seemed to be the main cook, prepared a delicious meal of mushrooms in a pepper and sour cream sauce, sautéed potatoes lightly spiced and some rather tasty soya cheese toast. After our meal, he brought in his guitar and sang some delightful songs, some folk and some his own. We all sat on their large sofa, with Vilma the Alsatian and little Roni curled up on our feet. They are a very fine family.

On my last teaching day, I brought in champagne, vodka, soft drinks, red caviar and other spreads with rye bread, and disposable cups and plates, and laid them out on one side of the classroom. We played various games, and in the most advanced class I decided to try 'Just a Minute' once again. As I mentioned in Chapter 17, Russian students were very hesitant about competing with one another openly.

However, I explained that to compete without rancour or self-congratulation could be fun. They got off to a slow start, but after one brave student dared to challenge a speaker, things began to hot up. By the end of the lesson the challenges were coming thick and fast and the students admitted that they had thoroughly enjoyed the experience.

Vladimir invited me to 'tea' the next day at 7.00 and told me that Valya and Genio would also be there. I was beginning to get into the swing of making my farewells: it no longer seemed so uncomfortable. So I also decided to call on my first landlords, Olga and Vitaly, the next morning.

I woke at five and lay in bed listening hopefully for the sound of rushing – or even dammit, trickling – water from the bath taps which were constantly left on in hopes. There wasn't so much as a drop in the bath, and my beloved landlord had used up several of my 5-litre bottles of water. It was another steaming hot day. I bought a bagful of cherries and raspberries and took a tram to Vitaly and Olga's. Olga welcomed me warmly, despite the fact that this was my first visit in many months. So did their black dog, Chorny. Vitaly, however, barely acknowledged my presence and pottered about in the yard. Olga brought a small table and stool out into the yard and left me to sit quietly and peacefully in the shade while she prepared some food. When she returned with food and a bottle of chilled champagne, I was delighted to see that she laid out three plates: this meant that Vitaly was included in the feast. But when she called him, I had to tell her that he had left on his bike some minutes earlier.

To my relief, Vitaly returned about ten minutes later and joined us. After a few mouthfuls of one of Olga's delicious cakes, Vitaly visibly relaxed and became chatty. He gave me an odd cherry from the bag I'd given them: it had a tiny 'twin' attached to one end, and he told me it represented Paul and Lena (the latter being quite small).

Then a rather friendly chicken from next door bustled into the yard and promptly laid a very small and odd-shaped egg, like a teeny pear. Vitaly insisted that I take that, too. (Indeed, I still have it!) He also found a little lidded pot to put these treasures in, and Olga contributed some cotton wool. It was so nice to see these two intelligent people behaving lovingly and trustfully. Visiting them, I said, was like bringing my Russian experience full circle. Eventually, I bade them an affectionate farewell and inwardly prayed that life would treat them with tenderness.

'Tea' with Luda and Vladimir consisted of tiny new potatoes, dishes of fresh herbs, several delicious salads, thin slices of cheese, an excellent red wine from the Krasnodar region and, finally, a mouth-watering chocolate cake with Earl Grey tea.

Valya told me that Jonathan was looking pink-cheeked and triumphant after his first few mixed classes. I was so glad to hear this, both on account of my students and on Jonathan's own account. It would do wonders, I was sure, for his confidence. I guess, being much older than him and a strong character to boot, I might unwittingly have 'blocked' him a bit.

Now he would be the sole teacher in charge.

Both Valya and I were exhausted, but in that haven we were permitted to be so. My head was dizzy and buzzing and I suspect that, on occasion, I dozed between mouthfuls.

When I rose to leave, I was presented with a beautiful samovar and it was all I could do not to burst into tears. On arriving home, I found a note from Tolik asking if he could come round with some friends that evening.

My heart sank temporarily. Though it may not seem like it, I am naturally a bit of a loner and delight in quiet times on my own. But the weather had cooled down, and there was no way I was going to disappoint Tolik, who had been a good friend to me.

When he appeared to check whether I had received his note, he rather mysteriously asked me to give him a photo of myself, which I did, and he shot off.

Before he returned, his wife Olya arrived, and immediately confessed that Tolik was preparing a surprise for me. I could see she was about to spill the beans – Russians find it terribly difficult to keep secrets! – but then she pursed her lips and said she mustn't say anything. I gave her a drink and we chatted amicably on the balcony. There had just been a heavy downpour and everything smelt gloriously wet and earthy. A golden oriole flew into the poplar in the yard and sang its thanks for water.

Tolik returned, looking hassled and pink-faced. He admitted he had been hunting for his friend Andrei Round Eyes, but could not find him. Andrei was very clever at creating images on computer, and I suspected that Tolik had wanted him to create a card of some kind, incorporating the picture I had given him. I could see that Tolik was frightfully upset that he had nothing to give me, and I so wanted to reassure him that it really did not matter. His affection was what was important to me. Galya arrived at about ten, followed shortly after by Andrei Round Eyes. We all began to relax and enjoy ourselves. I asked Andrei if he could make my printer safe for the journey. In true Russian fashion, he wrapped it beautifully, care of two plastic bags, some of my cellotape, and the flex of the printer!

We agreed that we would miss one another very much. The fact that we had met precisely six times in one and a half years was of no account. He told me that I was his 'window on the world' and that made me happy. From time to time, one meets someone who is instantly so familiar that you know you have met before – not in this life, evidently, but in a previous incarnation. Andrei was such a one to me. He presented me with a calendar he had designed, which ended in March 2000, and said he would tell me everything when I returned to Taganrog once the calendar reached its end. Sadly, I did not return, but I often send him thoughts of love and hope.

When they all finally left in the early hours, I fell into bed, exhausted, yet happy.

33 Farewell Russia

I woke early, and walked down to the sea at 7.00 am for a cool bathe. The tide was quite high, and there was a glowing morning light on the sea, already busy with bobbing fishing boats.

I returned to complete my final packing and take any rubbish to the bins. At about 3.00 pm, Jonathan turned up to say goodbye. While he was still there, my ghastly landlord arrived and plonked himself territorially on the best armchair in the living room. When Jonathan lit up, he aggressively ordered him to go out onto the balcony. I was delighted that Jonathan, usually given to timidity, stood his ground and quietly told Alexandr that he wasn't very polite.

Genio and Valya, who had insisted on driving me to Rostov station, arrived promptly at four. Alexandr immediately accosted Valya and demanded money to replace the kalonka (gas water heater). He had never mentioned anything to me, though he had been working in the bathroom for several days. It did indeed look pretty black and rotten when he removed the cover, but that was his responsibility. Valya just ignored him, and he followed her round the flat, waving his stick and yelling curses. She calmly retorted that he could send letters of complaint to the bloody White House if he chose. He then turned on me and demanded the key. I told him I would hand it over when I left, and not a moment before. Fortunately, I had had the sense to put the key in my pocket, the moment he arrived. After checking that everything had been taken out to the car, I handed him the key. His last word to Valya and me, as we thankfully closed the door on him, was 'Swines!' I silently prayed that he would no longer plague poor Valya, though frankly, I think he had met his match there.

The drive to Rostov was miserable. We were all tired, and sad about leave-taking. At the station, I bought drinks and ice creams for us all. I also wanted to buy Genio a bottle of Scotch, but Valya threw a fit of hysterics, crying that it cost the same as her month's salary. I decided that purchasing it would cause more pain than pleasure, so plumped for some chocolates – which probably melted in the car on their drive home. Both Valya and I burst into tears as we said goodbye.

My travelling companions on the Tikki Don Train were delightful. Vika was a 19-year-old student from Rostov, and Sergei, an army major, was returning to Kalinin from a visit to his mother in the Ukraine. He told me he and his men had not been paid for months.

Language Link had assigned me a teacher's flat on the outskirts of Moscow, and also sent me a driver, who picked me up from the station and gave me my air ticket. They certainly looked after their teachers.

However, when I looked at my ticket, having made myself a cup of tea, I was shocked to see that it cost US$863. Had they bought me an Executive Ticket? I frantically checked what cash I had, and realised I didn't have nearly enough. After a moment's initial panic, I checked my diary. Yes, just as I remembered, Marina in the Moscow office had given me the ticket details over the phone, and had cited a top price of US$388. There had to be some mistake.

I took the metro to the central office next morning. Natasha, in her soft, calm voice, instantly reassured me. "They do that sometimes," she said. "I don't know why. We paid 388 dollars and that's what you owe us. Anyway, we just don't have that sort of money lying around." After settling up, I spent a very pleasant hour chatting to Natasha in the kitchen over coffee. She was an extremely intelligent and efficient woman, skillful with people, tough when necessary, and with a heart as big as a Russian samovar. She told me she was going to Dublin later in the year, and I said

I was sure she would love it there as she would find the Irish very much to her liking. This interested her, and she admitted that she had always thought her Irish boss was very different from all the English people she had met. "'You know, Gilli," she said, "he thinks of people and what they need first. Money isn't really important to him. And he's so generous." Yes. I had heard this about him, too. Finally, Natasha told me there would always be a job for me in Russia, if I needed one. That made my heart glad.

I then took the metro – changing stations at whim, just to enjoy the individuality of each – to the Arbat, where I had a most successful shop, finding suitable presents for my loved ones at home. After a meal in a little back street restaurant, I took a leisurely stroll through winding streets to Morskaya and beyond. I do love Moscow. It seems to have developed in a fairly random fashion – like London, and unlike St Petersburg – so that the grand, the homely, the beautiful and the ugly, the old and new and the merely mundane are all jostled together. It makes for an interesting combination.

There was a tremendous storm in the night. Nearly an hour of sheet lightning and rolls of thunder with extremely heavy rain. I sat on the balcony of the flat and watched the aerial display. Windows lit up, then darkened, in the nine-storey block opposite, like a movie theatre. There was a mother, holding and reassuring a frightened child; an old babushka, shawl-wrapped, disapprovingly closed her window and drew the curtains; a beautiful, apparently naked young man, sat by his window gazing thoughtfully out at the battling sky. Three teenagers, daring one another to lean far out at a window, shrieked with excitement and fear. I was going to miss this communal lifestyle.

Farewell dear Russia!

Epilogue

Though I have not returned to Taganrog since July 1999, I have visited Russia twice since then, to visit my friends Ina and Vova and their son, who is my godson. They moved first to Cmolensk, an interesting old town in the north-west, and then to a country town 50 km south of St Petersburg. St P. is delightful in the summer, and I enjoyed wandering its streets. Though the large international cities are modernized and much altered since the 1990s, the lesser-known country towns seem little different from the Taganrog I got to know in many respects, though grand new houses bear witness to the growing spread of capitalism.

I met up with Valya every summer for a number of years, when she accompanied students to a language school in Oxford, and later discovered that Galya had married a Norwegian and lived in Norway.

As for Roman! Well, I always knew he would get around some. He contacted me one day to say he was in London, and I met him there, and then invited him to spend a weekend with me in Colchester.

He had moved to Moscow, married a Russian girl, had a daughter, divorced, and was now working in London. I later introduced him to an ex-student of mine from Bulgaria, they fell in love and married. They now have a son and baby daughter.

Paul and Lena settled in London, and have two delightful children.

I get news of some of my ex-students via Roman and perhaps one day I shall revisit Taganrog, though I know that a large proportion of the students I taught have since left Taganrog for other parts of Russia or other countries. Whether or not, that little town in south-west Russia will always have a special place in my heart. And there are many people there to whom I send my warmest love and thanks for their friendship. May they thrive.

In conclusion, I offer my heartfelt thanks to my friend Sreeram Iyer, without whose technical help I could not have "self-published" this book.

Printed in Great Britain
by Amazon